CASE STUDIES IN
CULTURAL ANTHROPOLOGY

GENERAL EDITORS
George and Louise Spindler
STANFORD UNIVERSITY

THE BOLIVIAN AYMARA

make vocab. list

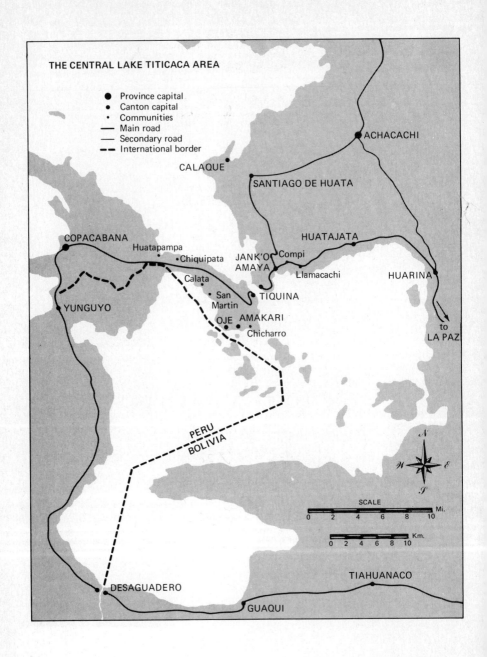

THE CENTRAL LAKE TITICACA AREA

- Province capital
- Canton capital
- Communities
— Main road
— Secondary road
-- International border

ACHACACHI

CALAQUE

SANTIAGO DE HUATA

COPACABANA

Huatapampa

Chiquipata

HUATAJATA

JANK'O AMAYA

Compi

Calata

Llamacachi

HUARINA

San Martin

TIQUINA

YUNGUYO

OJE AMAKARI

Chicharro

to LA PAZ

PERU
BOLIVIA

N
W   E
S

SCALE

Mi.
0   2   4   6   8   10

Km.
0   2   4   6   8   10

TIAHUANACO

DESAGUADERO

GUAQUI

THE BOLIVIAN AYMARA

By

HANS C. BUECHLER

Syracuse University

and

JUDITH-MARIA BUECHLER

Syracuse University and LeMoyne College

HOLT, RINEHART AND WINSTON, INC.

NEW YORK   CHICAGO   SAN FRANCISCO   ATLANTA

DALLAS   MONTREAL   TORONTO   LONDON   SYDNEY

Cover: *Manuel*

Foreword

About the Series

These case studies in cultural anthropology are designed to bring to students, in beginning and intermediate courses in the social sciences, insights into the richness and complexity of human life as it is lived in different ways and in different places. They are written by men and women who have lived in the societies they write about and who are professionally trained as observers and interpreters of human behavior. The authors are also teachers, and in writing their books they have kept the students who will read them foremost in their minds. It is our belief that when an understanding of ways of life very different from one's own is gained, abstractions and generalizations about social structure, cultural values, subsistence techniques, and the other universal categories of human social behavior become meaningful.

About the Authors

Hans C. Buechler is an assistant professor of Anthropology at Syracuse University. He grew up in Bolivia and Switzerland and received his graduate training in anthropology at the Sorbonne, Paris, and at Columbia University. He holds a Ph.D. from Columbia University and has taught at the Université de Montréal. He is co-author of the book *Land Reform and Social Revolution in Bolivia* with D. Heath and C. Erasmus, and is currently preparing a book on the relationships between rural and urban Aymara fiestas and social networks.

Judith-Maria Buechler is an instructor of Anthropology at University College, Syracuse University and at LeMoyne College. She grew up in China, Haiti, and the United States. She received an M.A. in anthropology from Columbia University and is currently preparing her Ph.D. thesis on Aymara marketing for McGill University. She has taught at Queen's College, Monmouth College, and Marianapolis College, Montreal.

About the Book

In this case study dealing with the Bolivian Aymara, the focus is on the inhabitants of Compi, a community on the shores of Lake Titicaca on the Bolivian high plateau. The inhabitants of Compi usually view Compi as a geographically definable unit, but, like other peasant communities, it must be viewed as a part of a complex system with reference to the wider social, temporal, and spatial framework. This is exactly what the Buechlers have done. They have furnished the reader with an important historical summary of the community and deal with activities that occur within the set boundaries plus those that occur when the Compeños travel and migrate to the city of La Paz. Compeños themselves give formal recognition to their wider ties by including dance groups composed of migrants in their fiestas and by placing returned migrants in positions of authority.

The authors emphasize the great variety of situations existing among the Aymara. In this respect, the community of Compi was an excellent choice as it provides an example of both former landed estates and free communities. Actually, Compi is composed of five communities, each with its own identity. Thus, the study affords a good representation of widely divergent patterns.

The fieldworkers saw the results of an agrarian reform which occurred in 1953, transforming the peasants from serfs to landholders. Thus the account of the community's history in Chapter 1 is essential to understanding the ties between Compi families and the complex community structure comprised of former estates in the hacienda system. The authors summarize materials from the time of Inca domination through the period of the Spanish lords and the hacienda system and the agrarian reform of 1953, pointing out continuities existing throughout the various periods.

In the chapter on economic organization, the Buechlers describe drastic changes which have occurred with peasant participation in the distribution and consumption of goods since 1953. The change has been from an incipient market economy in which the Indian participated primarily on the village level with *mestizo* intermediaries to a market system in which the Indian participates on both the village and the city levels. A detailed account of how the marketing system works, with women taking the major roles, is given. A complex relationship exists between producer, middleman, vendors, and consumers which is determined by one's *cacera* ties. These are reciprocal relationships whereby a person maintains a regular clientele by providing set services and better quality merchandise at a cheaper price and/or credit. One's *cacera* ties and credit rating increase as one's social network expands. The authors provide firsthand insight into these relationships through the use of case materials and life histories, illustrating the kinds of problems the market women face.

The authors have gathered elaborate materials on the fiesta system, which includes a system of sponsorship, or cargos, widespread in Latin America. Through the use of rich case materials the Buechlers trace the route specific individuals take in ascending the hierarchy of the cargo system.

The Buechlers enliven their discussion of the Compi family and Compi politics with descriptions of specific individuals engaged in various activities. The community meetings are characterized by conflict—endless disputes centering around land distribution and ownership and regulation of the school. Most of the conflict originates between the Compeños and peasants who were not historically a part of the hacienda system. It is only because of the complex network of kinship ties that exist between the groups that any form of cooperation is possible at times. Family ties play an important role also in relating the migrant to the village. There is constant visiting between families in the city and the village.

In the concluding chapter, where the authors compare the lives of Compeños with those of other Aymara, they write that ". . . the anthropologist must go beyond artificial self-imposed geographic, social, ethnic, and temporal boundaries . . . [and] must follow the network of social relationships through time and space."

The Buechlers have applied the concept of social networks (Barnes 1968) in measuring the expression of regularities in interpersonal interaction. The Aymara situation yields rich data for the application of this concept.

LOUISE AND GEORGE SPINDLER
General Editors

Phlox, Wisconsin
1970

Preface

Recent developments in the anthropology of peasant communities stress the fact that such communities must be seen as parts of complex systems rather than in isolation. The inhabitants of Compi, a community on the shores of Lake Titicaca on the Bolivian high plateau, are able to show the visitor territorial boundaries which encompass most of their land. In this sense Compi appears to be a definable unit. In order to understand the activities and preoccupations of Compeños, however, it is insufficient to study only the activities within these boundaries. Today we may find a Compeño working in his fields or attending a community fiesta, but tomorrow he may be purchasing goods at the weekly fair, attending a bullfight, or bringing a dispute in front of the judge in the county capital. The next day he may sell dried meat in the tropical Yungas valleys or onions in La Paz, the capital of Bolivia, where he may stay at the home of relatives who have migrated permanently to La Paz.

Even the activities of the Compeños within the territorial boundaries of the community cannot be understood without reference to a wider social, temporal, and spatial framework. One part of the community was a landed estate or hacienda until the agrarian reform of 1953, which transformed the peasants from serfs to landholders. A few years later the landlord, who had completely dominated the lives of these Compeños, disappeared from the scene completely. As a matter of fact, the very structure of the community with its multiple subdivisions can only be understood with reference to its complex history in which outside factors have played a dominant role. This does not mean, however, that Compi was the mere pawn of outside influence shaping it in haphazard fashion through the vagaries of history. On the contrary, many Aymara cultural patterns seem to have persisted through the centuries. This, however, seems to be due to their adaptability to new situations rather than because of any inherent traditionalism.

The concept of social network is one of the new tools for analyzing cases where traditional anthropological methods geared toward the study of territorially bounded units have proven inadequate. J. A. Barnes (1954) coined the term in his analysis of a Norwegian parish to account for far-flung ties across territorial and even social group boundaries. Subsequently, the concept has been used for example, to describe politics in India (Bailey 1963), conjugal role patterns in London (Bott 1955), and economics and politics among Ecuadorian and Nova Scotian Blacks (Whitten 1970). Network analysis presupposes no social or cultural boundaries. It is simply a means to plot direct and indirect ties between human beings. An anthropologist may begin his analysis by plotting all the ties established by one of his informants with other individuals. He may then study the ties connecting these individuals among themselves and with persons other than the initial informant, and so on (see Barnes 1968). The limits of his inquiry may simply be dictated by practical considerations. He may, for instance, include any sort of interpersonal ties within two or three network links from his initial informant, or he may narrow his inquiry to ties established for or influencing a specific activity, for example, marketing agricultural produce, creating a political following, or obtaining aid in cultivating land.

He may search for regularities in the network segment he has plotted. Thus, he may study what proportion of individuals who maintain ties with the initial informant in turn maintains ties among themselves; in other words, he may analyze what Barnes calls the "density" of a network segment. To give one example, he may find that persons who buy produce from and sell it to each other maintain few common ties with other persons and thus form a loose network segment, while close bilateral kin form a dense one. He may also analyze regularities in the persons who initiate action (see Chapple and Coon 1942) and how orders or information are passed on from individual to individual in the network or regularities in the manner in which new ties are established. Finally, he may analyze regularities in the ways in which interpersonal ties change over time.

Network analysis leads to a different view of "groups" and "institutions." Rather than natural units of analysis which need no further explanation, they appear as regularities in network segments which have received formal recognition through law, ideology, ritual, or other symbolic means. From the point of view of network analysis, all "groups" and "institutions" must be seen in the context of the wider network. "Groups" and "institutions" are but one aspect of network regularities, however, for not all network regularities are given equal formal recognition by a society, and, thus, the study of "institutions" and named "groups" must be complemented by a search for other network regularities. In this book the concept of social network underlies our analysis of Compi family, community, and county organization as well as our discussion of marketing and migration.

Finally, network analysis is a useful tool to measure the process whereby societies express regularities in interpersonal relations. The Aymara fiesta system and religion are two such means of symbolic expression which we shall analyze.

We carried out fieldwork among the Aymaras between 1961 and 1969. In 1961 Hans Buechler acted as an assistant to William Carter in an Aymara community study. In the summer of 1963 he returned for a survey on landed estates affected by the agrarian reform of 1953 supported by the Land Tenure Center, University of Wisconsin. In November 1964 he initiated fieldwork in Compi under a Columbia Travelling Fellowship and later under a project jointly sponsored by the Research Institute for the Study of Man and the Peace Corps (Grant No. PC (W)-397). In June 1965 Judith-Maria Buechler joined him in the field, and both remained there until February 1966. He carried out a general community study with particular reference to the social effects of land reform and migration while she studied the activities of the women and children in general with an emphasis on childhood from the prenatal period through adolescence. In the summer of 1967 Judith-Maria Buechler made a study of market women, including Compi migrants in La Paz, as a grantee of the McGill University Center for Developing Area Studies. Hans Buechler studied fiestas both in Compi and in La Paz under a Canada Council grant. In the summer of 1969 the authors returned to Bolivia, aided by the Social Science Research Council and the Center for Developing Area Studies of McGill University to study political networks, market syndicates, and marketing on the altiplano and in La Paz.

We wish to thank our interpreters Paz Nacho and Sofía Velazquez as well as our many informants in Compi, Llamacachi, and La Paz. We would also like to express our gratitude to our *compadre* Dr. Alexander G. Moore for his detailed and thoughtful comments on the manuscript. This book is dedicated to our twin daughters Simone and Stephanie.

H. B.

J.-M. B.

Contents

Dancer at a Compi folklore festival

Girl and orange in Capilaya

View of Compi proper from Cawaya

1

Introduction

The Setting

COMPI IS SITUATED on the central shores of Lake Titicaca. The community can be reached from La Paz, the capital of Bolivia, by the Panamerican Highway. La Paz is one of the two major destinations of the "out-migrants," and a center through which all migrants to another migration zone, the Yungas valleys, must pass.

Starting out on the high plateau or "altiplano" from La Paz at eight o'clock in the morning, this road is a series of dust clouds flying away at an angle over the sweeping plateau. The trucks and buses leave La Paz at seven in the morning, or earlier, in order to arrive at the Straits of Tiquina, 100 kilometers[1] from La Paz, between 9 and 10 A.M., the time when propitious winds fill the sails of the wooden barges which carry them across the lake to the peninsula of Copacabana.

After a climb out of the basin of La Paz, the highway continues as a wide dirt road which is rather well maintained by Alliance for Progress graders. On either side of the road, peasant houses each surrounded by large house plots, ranging in size from 2 to 50 hectares,[2] lie in loose clusters separated from other clusters by vast tracts of land. Every 10 kilometers or so one passes settlements which are more nucleated, and usually of recent origin. Aymara peasants built them after the agrarian reform in order to fulfill the needs of a rapidly expanding market network and rural administration.

After 60 kilometers, one reaches the old Spanish town of Huarina from whence the road continues to Achacachi, the province capital, situated 15 kilometers from Huarina.

At this junction, the road branching off to Copacabana follows Lake Titicaca. It narrows considerably and becomes more jolting. Here population is denser, concentrated in the lower parts of valleys along the hilly shore. Recently, many peasants have built their houses along the road for easy access to transportation to

---

[1] A kilometer is ⅝ of a mile.
[2] A hectare contains 2.47 acres.

1

regional fairs and to La Paz. Some 20 kilometers from Huarina one reaches Huatajata, where for many decades the Canadian Baptists have maintained a mission which built the first schools in the area, including the first school in Compi and in Llamacachi. Only half an hour away by bicycle or 20 minutes by truck, the mission in Huatajata also runs the nearest infirmary available to Compeños.

Near Huatajata is the area's high school, little used by Compeños who prefer to go to La Paz if they desire a higher education.

After Huatajata one travels through a number of ex-haciendas until one reaches Llamacachi. The borderline between Llamacachi and Chua, the last one of these ex-haciendas, is a little stream which flows through and irrigates a small fertile valley. During hacienda times, that is, before the agrarian reform, there were frequent disputes with Chua over the water rights of this brook. Most of Llamacachi, however, lies on a well-sheltered but rather steep hill to the right of the road and on the fertile lake shore, a site unfortunate in that the lake level rises periodically and swallows almost all of these shore lands. Llamacachi has only 75 hectares of agricultural land to feed its 308 inhabitants, and much of this land spreads over a stony hillside which has to lie fallow for many years in order to regain its fertility. Llamacacheños, however, have access to spacious pasture lands extending into the surrounding hills which belong to neighboring Compi. Compeños are uninterested in exploiting these pasture lands to their full capacity and therefore permit free use of them to all neighboring communities.

Compi itself is composed of five sections or subzones with 1230 inhabitants in all. Each section has its own identity, even though all belonged to one patrón for many decades.

The road first traverses a valley, some 400 meters wide. This is Compi proper. About 1.3 kilometers inland the valley seems to end, but it continues behind a high embankment. A number of houses, rising up the steep slopes like the rows of seats in an amphitheater, border the end of the valley. This area is always green due to a number of springs arising higher up on the mountain that supply four of the five sections with water for irrigation. Here is the section called Cawaya.

A hill separates Compi from Capilaya which is green the year round too, because it shares the spring water with Cawaya and Compi. Tuaca, in turn separated from Capilaya by a low hill on which the cemetery of all five sections lies, is less fortunate with its water supply. Only part of it can be irrigated by a long canal to the spring. At Tauca the road turns at a right angle and reaches Amasi, really a section of Compi proper, but somewhat isolated from the main stream of Compi life. The last section belonging to Compi is Kalamaya, the smallest of all the sections and the only one without any irrigation.

Between the road and the lake, from the border with Llamacachi to Kalamaya, there is a broad strip of land, some 90 hectares, which was the patrón's most productive land. The history of this land is a most fascinating example of Compi land tenure up to the present day, for it reflects the patrón's increasing control over hacienda resources and its decline after the agrarian reform.

The houses in Compi and Llamachachi are dispersed over the valley floors and lower parts of the hill slopes. Each domicile is surrounded by one of the many scattered plots owned by each peasant. However, more and more *campesinos* are building houses on the road if they happen to own a plot of land there, or if they have been able to exchange a parcel of land for one bordering the road, because onions are now grown on a large scale in the community as a cash crop and are marketed by each grower in La Paz, the capital. A house near the road enables the peasants to keep an eye on the large bundles of onions that are to be taken by truck to La Paz.

Llamacachi, the free community studied intensively, occupies a small section of the lake shore squeezed in between Compi and Chua, another large former hacienda. Like Compi, it is strongly dependent on onions for an income and is too crowded to accommodate the younger generation.

History

The Compi area has been inhabited for centuries by Aymara-speaking Indians, who originally formed a number of chiefdoms or small kingdoms. Later these shared the fate of most Andean peoples. After a period of Inca domination they were conquered by the Spaniards and held in virtual serfdom. First they were given away in *encomienda*, or protectorate, to Spanish colonists who thereby demanded tribute in exchange for protection. This tribute was supposed to be paid in cash or in kind. In actual fact, however, many Aymara chiefdoms continued to follow the Inca practice of paying tribute in the form of labor. The communities set aside land on which to grow crops and raise llamas and alpacas with which to pay the dues both to the *curaca* or chief, and to the *encomendero*, or Spanish lord. Furthermore peasants often had to perform work for the *encomenderos* who at the same time were landowners. Land was also distributed by the authorities apart from the *encomienda* and was frequently held without valid titles. From the 1650s onward, the Spanish Crown, motivated by its need for money and a desire to reorder this state of affairs, confirmed such titles on a large scale. In this way large estates were created and confirmed, with some owners from the *encomienda* category and some not. With regard to the labor supply, there was a system called *repartimiento* by which the Indians were assigned to the Spaniards to work for low wages, which were paid into communal treasuries. In practice, the *corregidores*, or judges who governed the Indian communities and the Crown, were the sole beneficiaries of these treasuries. The labor in the mines in Potosi was supplied in this way, giving rise to a high mortality and much suffering among the Indians. Since the *repartimiento* system was most unsatisfactory for the landowners, they attempted to attract many of the Indians who had escaped from the mines or other obligations to settle down on the landed estates, or haciendas. While the *encomienda* declined and finally disappeared early in the eighteenth century, haciendas proliferated. Bolivia's independence from Spain in 1825 further increased their number and size, for the Indian communities lost even the little protection they had previously enjoyed from the Crown. Thus, in 1952, only 3783 free communities were left in the entire country and many of these were small and overpopulated.

The hacienda system on the high plateau was essentially a system of serfdom in which peasants both worked for a certain number of days per week for landlords and rendered certain services in return for the use of a few parcels of land. The manner in which the haciendas were administrated followed the same principles of organization as the communities who had succeeded in retaining their independence. Similar to peasants in free communities, the serfs' usufruct rights were usually inherited from father to son. The landlords reserved the right to reallocate land as they wished, but they only rarely took advantage of this privilege. In many haciendas overseers were appointed in the same way as the authorities in free communities, that is, following a hierarchy of prestige based on feast sponsorship as well as on civic obligations. The duties of hacienda serfs were often severe. In the central Lake Titicaca area as many as 12-man labor days per week were required per family. In addition, the *colono* families took turns herding the landlord's sheep and cattle, doing the cooking, transporting produce, and so on.

Free communities were not exempt from obligations to the conquering class even after the *repartimiento* system, including forced labor in the mines, was abolished. Apart from the annual taxes collected from each family by the community head, or *jilakata,* the colonial custom of providing the *mestizo* judge, or *corregidor,* with cheap produce continued. The peasants were forced to sell him eggs and meat at below-market prices. Furthermore, the *comunidades* under the *corregidor's* jurisdiction took turns sending him a servant for a period of one week at a time. This obligation extended to the parish priest as well. Finally, whenever necessary, *comunarios* repaired the plaza of the county capital where the *corregidor* resided. Every Sunday *jilakatas* met with the *corregidor* which often meant a walk of 10 miles or more; in addition, on the day of the major fiesta in the county capital, they sponsored a dance group composed of members of their communities. Also, they had to provide lodgings for the *corregidor* on his occasional rounds of the communities under his jurisdiction and his transportation on mule back to his next destination.

These harsh conditions prevailed until 1952–1953 when they were finally alleviated. In April 1952 the Movimiento Nacional Revolucionario, a progressive political party, gained control of the government of Bolivia and decreed a series of laws in favor of Aymara peasants culminating in the agrarian reform laws of August 1953. These laws not only abolished all unremunerated labor but provided for the division of most of the land held by estate owners among their former *colonos* as well.

The central Lake Titicaca area where Compi is located is a mosaic of former landed estates and free communities. Most of the latter are situated in the interstices between haciendas or occupy particularly rough terrain. Since all free communities are overpopulated, they depend on external sources for an income. In some the peasants rely on fishing for a subsidiary revenue, in others the men travel to the semi-tropical Yungas valleys with meat from the high plateau or buy coca in the tropics for sale in La Paz, while the women weave at home. In yet other communities the Indians work a few months per year, or even for years for peasants in the Yungas or in tin mines. Finally, many migrate temporarily or permanently to the cities.

Compi provides an example of both former landed estates and free communities. In effect, it is composed of a large former hacienda, itself subdivided into five semi-autonomous sections and parts of a free community. This *comunidad,* called Llamacachi, had encompassed most of Compi up to the second half of the nineteenth century when it was largely assimilated by the hacienda. Llamacachi has continued to maintain marriage ties with the rest of Compi and partakes in most Compi fiestas. In view of the multiple connections between Compi and Llamacachi it is useful to treat them together.

COMMUNITY HISTORY

In order to understand the intricate ties between Compi families and the complex community structure, typical of large former estates (and in many ways of all large Aymara communities), we must give a more detailed account of the community's history.

In the mid-nineteenth century, two of the five sections of Compi, Compi proper and Capilaya, constituted two separate haciendas with different owners. The other three sections of Compi, Tauca, Kalamaya, and Cawaya, all belonged to one large *comunidad,* called Tauca, which included Llamacachi. Compi proper and Capilaya later merged and grew by the accretion of *comunidad* land. This process continued until the turn of the century in spite of the desperate efforts of many *comunidad* peasants, or *comunarios,* to hold on to their land. Only Llamacachi and a handful of Tauca and Kalamaya peasants succeeded in maintaining their independence. Their struggle can be illustrated by the following incident which occurred around 1900.

Most *comunarios* had succumbed to the land-hungry patrón. Pressure mounted on those who held out. One night, the patrón was about to invade the house of Manuel Ramos. Hearing of this, Manuel quickly put on women's garb and thus escaped undetected to Achacachi, the province capital. There he asked for aid, returning to Tauca with both soldiers and a judge. The patrón was warned against any further abuses and the judge then appointed Manuel as *jilakata* of the community which had become leaderless. From that day on, no more sales of land to Compi occurred. Even today, one finds small enclaves of *comunarios* in Tauca, Kalamaya, and Cawaya.

Between 1889 and 1900 Llamacachi's other hacienda neighbor, Chua, also attempted to expand at the *comunidad's* expense. For a short time Chua was successful; all but one Llamacachi family sold out to Chua during this period. However, the Llamacacheños created so much trouble for their landlord that he finally sold most of their land back to them. This repurchase is the basis for a longstanding feud between the two most important Llamacachi families, one of which lent the other money to reacquire land. Later the lender wanted to confiscate the land from the debtor. Even today this affair has not been entirely forgotten and contributes to the lack of unity in this small community.

At about the same time, many Tauca, Kalamaya, and Cawaya peasants attempted to regain their land by force in a bitter revolt which lasted for two years and involved a number of other free communities in the area. The struggle was complicated by the fact that, as a result of an inheritance squabble, one heir to the hacienda Compi took the side of the *comunarios* against the *colonos*. Such quarrels were not rare on the altiplano. They are one of the roots of the traditional distrust with which *comunarios* and *colonos* view each other. Even the agrarian reform has not been able to obliterate this distrust entirely.

In the first half of this century conditions on the hacienda worsened steadily. Although the personal services to be rendered to the patrón remained much the same throughout decades and probably throughout centuries, the severity with which punishment was meted and the number of days per week the *colonos* were compelled to work for their landlord increased, as did the daily work hours. At the same time the amount of land allotted to each family decreased. Due to these deteriorating conditions a large number of *colonos* abandoned their hacienda. Some, who had married *comunarios,* moved to the plots of their parents-in-law, in an attempt to avoid their turn at some of the more time-consuming personal services which they were obligated to perform, returning only when the danger of being recruited was over. Others migrated to La Paz. Most have remained there although some returned just before and after the agrarian reform.

The history of Compi-Llamacachi underlines the need to view the community as a network of social relationships rather than as a territorially-bounded entity. Without a knowledge of the complex interaction between Llamacachi peasants, landlords, peasants from Compi and other neighboring haciendas, and migrants to La Paz, neither the community structure of Compi and Llamacachi nor present trends can be understood. The groundwork for post-reform cooperation in education, patterns of migration, as well as politics and factionalism, were laid in the pre-reform history of the network of social relations in which Compeños and Llamacacheños participate.

THE AGRARIAN REFORM

For the peasant in Compi, the decree of the second of August, 1953, meant —as it did for all haciendas on the high plateau and for the country as a whole— a social revolution, unparalleled in Bolivian history. Llamacachi and all other free communities were indirectly affected as well, for the changing social situation had a profound impact on the relationships between La Paz and the countryside.

The most significant changes brought about by the agrarian reform decree was the abolition of the hacienda system and the distribution of most of the former estate lands to the peasants who had worked them. Immediately after the reform the peasants gained full ownership rights for lands over which they had previously held usufruct rights in return for their services. Lands worked for the patrón were frequently distributed among the peasants as well. In some cases the landlords were allowed to retain up to 80 hectares (200 acres) of agricultural land plus pasture lands. Where the landlord desired to cultivate his land rather than to sell it to his former *colonos*, cash remuneration was theoretically obligatory. In actual fact, however, share-cropping arrangements were more usual on the altiplano.

The government and subsequent governments have attempted to improve agricultural techniques as well. One avenue taken to accomplish this was the formation of consumer and production cooperatives. However, these rarely proved successful. Other avenues were the creation of agricultural experimentation centers established with the help of foreign development agencies. Vast educational campaigns accompanied the changes in land ownership. Today there are schools in almost every altiplano community, many of which even provide adult education classes.

In Compi all unremunerated labor and services and all patronal control of plots cultivated by former *colonos* was abolished in a matter of a few months. After the agrarian reform and to an extent even before the reform, the hacienda system, now operating on a labor-remunerated basis, went through a period of steady decline before it disappeared altogether. During this time the lands previously cultivated for the landlord were worked on a part share-cropping and part salaried basis. Moreover, services which did not disappear altogether were paid for in cash. Although no acts of violence were committed in Compi itself, in the aftermath of the reform two members of the patrón's family were killed in other places. The remaining heir sold all the cattle. Some of the land which was still in his hands was expropriated in favor of the former *colonos*, the rest he sold to them individually after a period of working it as a cooperative with a group of ex-*colonos*. First the expropriated land was worked jointly, with part of the revenue being distributed, the rest earmarked for school construction. However, abuses were frequent and Compeños were soon disillusioned with the idea of any kind of cooperative. Today parcels are rented out to community members for a fixed annual rate.

In spite of mismanagement and outright absconding with community funds by migrants who had returned to the community from La Paz, Compi has managed—with the aid of a Catholic institution—to build a large school. It has become the pride of Compeños and an extremely important cohesive and motivating force in the community. Schools with their stress on civics (history) are also contributing toward giving Compeños a sense of national identity.

The social reforms of the 1950s gave the peasants a voice in politics. Political positions in the countryside such as county judgeships are now filled mostly by persons with peasant backgrounds. A man of peasant extraction even became a cabinet minister. Finally, Compeños have become involved more and more directly in the national economy. Local markets now provide consumer goods from all over the world. Each peasant family also sells its produce directly in La Paz or through middlemen who themselves are members of the community. In La Paz they strengthen their ties with Compeños who have migrated there permanently and who help them with their business transactions. They also come into contact with peasants and middlemen from all over Bolivia. Finally, the military service is enlarging young Compeños' horizons.

In the subsequent chapters we shall attempt to follow these changes both from the vantage point of the community as a whole and from that of individual Compi families, and attempt to discover regularities in Compi social structure which will provide insight into both continuity and change.

2

Economic Organization

For those Compeños who have not emigrated, agriculture is the main source of livelihood. They are fortunate enough to be able to count on a fairly good climate for farming. The central Lake Titicaca area possesses the most favorable conditions for agriculture on the entire Bolivian high plateau. In this area the growing season, which begins in October farther south on the open plateau, sets in by September. Here too, there seems to be less danger of frost during crucial periods in plant growth although, like elsewhere on the high plateau, hail is a constant menace. All the major altiplano crops like potatoes, *ocas* (*Oxalis crenata*) and *isañu* (*Tropaeolum tuberosum*), two tubers of different families which both taste something like sweet potatoes, broad beans, or *habas*, barley, *papa liza* or *ullucu* (*Ullucus tuberosum*)—a tuber which looks like a brightly colored potato—and *quinua* (*Chenopodium quinoa*)—a cereal with very small but numerous grains, grow better here than elsewhere on the altiplano. Recently, onions have been introduced as a cash crop in the community.

Apart from these, other crops native to warmer climates grow here too. Peas, for instance, are planted among the broad beans. Even maize, which elsewhere grows only in temperate valleys up to an altitude of 3500 meters above sea level, can thrive here in sheltered spots around the lake.

The small valleys near the Straits of Tiquina are the most favored climatically, for these are protected from cold cordillera winds by hills ranging from 4000 to 4400 meters above sea level. Some of these valleys are even irrigable, permitting agriculture during the dry season, that is, between May and September. In Compi, for instance, there is a spring high up in the hills surrounding the community which permits the irrigation of two of its three valley bottoms. On its extensive though poor pasture lands up in the hills, Compi families herd small numbers of sheep and a few llamas. Preferring to invest their labor in agriculture, they under-utilize their pasture lands. Neighboring communities have profited from this lack of interest in animal husbandry in Compi to graze their sheep and llamas there. For their cattle, which they use for plowing, Compeños utilize the richer pastures in the upper reaches of the valleys and near the lake shore. The reeds and weeds that grow in the lake furnish valuable forage as well. Few Compeños fish although some own long rectangular nets which they extend at an angle to the shore to catch lake trout, a fish introduced by Peruvian hatcheries some 20 years ago. In contrast, other nearby communities depend to a considerable extent on trout and especially on smaller fish for a living. Compeños barter for the latter on the weekly market in the neighboring ex-hacienda. Trout are not consumed locally. They are destined for the markets in La Paz and for a small fish canning factory nearby. Fish is considered a delicacy in Compi. Compeños buy enough fresh fish for one meal for the entire family and salted and toasted fish for one or more additional meals per week. Aymaras eat meat (mutton and guinea pig) only on feast days and thus fish are their main sources of protein. Pork and eggs are also eaten occasionally although both are mainly destined for the city.

Compeños complement their revenues from agriculture with other activities. Most Compi families sell their own onions in La Paz. A handful also deal with onions from other community members, buy potatoes on local fairs for resale in La Paz or deal in contraband goods. Finally, a number of Compeños are carpenters, masons, and tailors, as well as cultivators. In spite of these specialties, however, agriculture continues to be the primary source of income.

Land Tenure and the Agricultural Cycle

As we have stated before, *colonos* had access to land on haciendas if they fulfilled certain services and performed a certain amount of labor per week. In Compi, four persons per family were required to work six days a week in return for the use of a full portion of land or *persona*.[1] Few families were blessed with the means to satisfy the stringent requirements of the hacienda and with surplus members of the family to cultivate a *persona*. Most worked half of a *persona*, i.e., a *media persona*.

One category of serfs, the *yanapacos*, worked somewhat less land than the *medias personas* and therefore had somewhat fewer obligations. Others, the *mayorunis*, tilled only a very small plot of land, completely insufficient for subsistence, for which they had to work only one day per week (*mayoruni* = *ma uruni* = of one day). The latter had to aid other peasants in order to gain a living. Some of these *mayorunis* and *yanapacos* were foreigners or persons who were living in the homes of other families.

The father of Silverio Sanchez from Capilaya, for instance, had came from the southern altiplano as a salt merchant. He had remained in Compi and herded sheep for the patrón, and as a compensation he received his plot of *mayoruni*.

Another person, named Fausto, had been working for the patrón as a servant. Fausto's father had fallen into disgrace with the patrón because he had been accused of losing a mule. His land was confiscated because he could not

---

[1] *Persona* literally means a person with the full responsibilities and rights of a household head and secondarily the land he cultivates.

make reparations. Fausto's mother returned to the hacienda to live with relatives while her son grew up with yet other relatives elsewhere. Later she recommended him to the patrón of the place where he lived as an adopted son. Since he was a peasant, his position was inferior to the patrón's own children, his status resembling that of an unsalaried servant. Later he ran away. When the patrón discovered where he was, he requested that he return to Compi and gave him the plot of *mayoruni*.

These different categories of *colonos* do not indicate the full extent of the ways in which access to land differed. Access to land varied considerably within each category as well. This was due to the fact that the fourfold classification into *personas, medias personas, yanapacos,* and *mayorunis* represented only one aspect of the system, namely the way in which the patrón and his aides assigned tasks to the *colonos.* The actual quantity of land a *colono* had access to depended not only on the category he belonged to, but also on inheritance patterns common to both *comunidades* and haciendas in the area, over which the patrón exercised little direct control. We shall deal with these patterns in the next chapter.

Pre-reform Agricultural Cycle

Previous to the agrarian reform the main crop in Compi seems to have been the potato which is, curiously enough, one of the least important crops in Compi today, and the crop which, at least during the year of our study, grew least well. Onions, which are now the most important crop, were attributed little importance then. Both onions and leeks were introduced some 30 or 40 years ago by Manuel Nacho, who had come as a wool dyer from Peru and had received land from the patrón. Later, other persons began to produce small quantities of onions, including the patrón himself who also raised other vegetables.

The agricultural cycle began with the sowing of *habas* in September. On the evening before the sowing, the hacienda overseers or *jilakatas* and their aides, the *alcaldes* proclaimed the event from a place near the center of each section; they reminded the people that one half of the families had to prepare their yokes of oxen and that the other half were obliged to appear at the hacienda house in order to help carry the seed out into the fields. At about seven o'clock in the morning the seed carriers would appear and the *jilakata* accompanied by the *mayordomo* and his peasant aide, the *sot'a* would order them to convey the seed to various fields. The *jilakatas* would have calculated the required seed amount for each field previously, so that the seed could be distributed accordingly.

For most agricultural tasks, Compi cooperated with Cawaya and Capilaya, while Tauca and Kalamaya formed another work group. Each group was responsible for certain sections of hacienda land.

In the fields the sacks of seed were emptied; after that, spoiled seed was separated from good seed. In the meantime, while the men who had brought plows started plowing, the men who had carried the seed worked with their hoes on the edges of the field which the plows could not reach. Their wives or other female members of their families sowed. For this purpose they received small sticks from the *jilakata* to measure the interval between seeds, as this had to be constant. Any variation from the norm was punished by the authorities who whipped any careless *colono* with an ornate silver whip, making him remove all seed from the wrongly sowed furrow and repeat the task. After each furrow was completed, there followed a short period of rest lasting until everybody had reached the end of his furrow; but apart from this, work continued uninterruptedly until noon.

Everyone, including the overseers and the administrator brought their lunch along and ate it in the field. Each laborer received a handful of coca,[2] the only remuneration under the hacienda system, and then toil continued until around 3:30 P.M., the hour of the *aculli*, when everyone ate the food they had reserved from lunch and chewed coca once more. The workday ended at 5 or 6 P.M., depending on the distance from the fields to the houses.

In the agricultural cycle the sowing of *ocas* came after the sowing of *habas*. This followed the same pattern. Formerly, about 40 to 60 *cargas*[3] of *ocas* were sown and later, in the time of the last patrón, this amount was increased to between 200 and 300 *cargas*. Similarly, in early times, after *oca* sowing, only about 80 *cargas* of potatoes were sown, although later this was increased to 300 or 400.

In contrast to that of other crops, potato sowing was a ceremonial occasion. A man, who played the *pinquillo* (a kind of flute) well, was asked to assemble a group of players. Once the field was reached, libations were offered to Mother Earth and to a few potatoes in a small cloth. These had been separated previously and had been covered with a handful of earth. Depending on whether the earth stuck to the potatoes when the cloth was opened, the next harvest was prognosticated as good or bad. The potatoes were then cut open and coca leaves and sheep's fat were stuck into the slit. These were the first potatoes to be sown. Then, after everybody had chewed coca and had drunk alcohol, the actual sowing would begin.

A month or two later, the *jilakata* proclaimed the beginning of cultivation and weeding. Families would then race each other to see who would be able to finish his furrow first. Afterwards, when all had completed the task, sometimes with the aid of those who worked faster and who took pity on their relatives who lagged behind, a new set of furrows was attacked. Cultivation and weeding ended soon after Candelaria (February 2d), the date at which Compeños cease to cultivate, since it is thought to be detrimental to the plants.

The next major event in the agricultural cycle was the *haba* harvest. Some 600 to 800 *quintals* (one *quintal* equals 100 pounds) of *habas* were harvested. Later the *quinua* was harvested and finally, starting after Easter, the potatoes and the *ocas*.

On the day of Corpus Christi (June 17th) threshing began. First the *quinua* had to be threshed. This was again a festive occasion. Three *yanapacos* and

---

[2] The coca leaf, often chewed with ashes containing lime, is a mild narcotic which numbs hunger sensation and produces some sense of well being. Some older Compeños consume a few handfuls a day. The younger ones chew it only on social and ritual occasions. In the one case we know, a habitual coca chewer who dropped the habit when he became a member of a Protestant sect, there seemed to have been no withdrawal symptoms. Most migrants in La Paz, especially men, stop chewing coca altogether.

[3] A carga is 162.7 pounds.

three *personas* from every section received *quinua* to make *chicha* (a fermented drink). Even sponsors were nominated for this day as in the big fiestas and sometimes the *jilakatas* were changed on this occasion.

Between San Juan (June 24th) and San Pedro (June 29th) the *habas* and barley were threshed. For this task a different work pattern than usual was adopted. The two work groups, Compi/Cawaya and Capilaya/Tauca/Kalamaya, worked alternating days and thus were free to help their relatives in the other group when it was their turn to thresh. Each family had to thresh a certain quantity per day, an amount which could not be achieved alone. For this purpose, even persons from Llamacachi and from Chua were invited to cooperate.

About the middle of June, when the weather on the altiplano is the coldest with strong frosts occurring during the night, about 20 boxes of potatoes, containing nine *cargas* each and a lesser amount of *ocas*, were given to an appointed family head, the *camani*, to make into *chuño*, frozen and dried potatoes, and *claya* (*ocas* elaborated in a similar fashion). The *camani* had to go about his task very carefully without wasting any potatoes or *ocas*. If less *chuño* or *claya* resulted than one third of the weight of the fresh tubers, he was compelled to add it of his own supply. To insure payment of the missing *chuño*, the patrón would ascertain that his *camanis* owned animals which could be expropriated if the need arose. If the harvest was plentiful, the *camani* would not be able to manage all this work by himself so he had to request aid from his relatives whom he had to pay himself. If the harvest was normal he could finish by Carmen (July 15th); if it was exceptionally good he sometimes had to continue until Rosario (the first Sunday in October).

By the end of June, after the harvest was brought in, many tasks still remained to be completed until the beginning of the next agricultural cycle. The hacienda house and the walls encircling the *ahijadero*, or pasture lands, needed to be repaired. The irrigation canals had to be cleaned and soon *habas*, potatoes and barley could be sown in places with irrigation and along the moist shores of the lake.

Parallel to the agricultural cycle there were also the various activities associated with cattle raising. For instance, from May to San Juan (June 24th) in the lake-shore pasture lands, the lambs were born. Then around San Andres (November 30th) they had to be separated from their mothers and brought to the hillside *ahijadero* where the males and ewes were segregated and tended by two shepherds, a service which *colono* families performed in turns of six months. At the same time the pregnant ewes were brought to the lake shore.

In the meantime the ewes whose lambs had been taken away from them were milked for the first time. The milker, who served for one week, would bring with him his family or those who liked the curd which was later distributed among the milkers. The milker fed all his helpers—sometimes as many as 15 of them. If he did not hand over the required quantity of milk, he was sometimes forced to fill the quota from his own sheep. This was not unusual, especially during the wettest weeks when the sheep generally produced less milk. The *sot'a* then put the rennet into the milk and formed three or four large white cheeses which were renowned for their good quality.

In the beginning of February, the castrated male sheep and the black or spotted sheep were being fattened in the choice pasture land along the streams. Later, around Easter when milking ended, the old ewes were added to this herd. Then, between Ascension and Corpus Christi, the animals were sold either to *colonos* or, more frequently, to peasants from Huatajata who butchered them and jerked the meat for sale in the Yungas. At the time when barley was being threshed, the castrated and the old pigs, some 180 in all, were separated from the herd of cattle which was tended by the *islero*, who served for six months. Then the pigs were fattened on barley and small *ocas* and potatoes in a corral. Next, between June and September, they were sold to the dealers from Huatajata. Another shepherd herded the old cows which were sold to be butchered, while the young bulls were all sold for plowing. The patrón himself kept only one bull, since the *colonos* had to furnish all plowing animals.

It is therefore not surprising that the women say that the family was more united and that the members of a family cooperated more in hacienda times; without such cooperation it would not have been possible for *colono* families to handle the tremendous load of hacienda labor in addition to cultivating their own fields.

POST-REFORM AGRICULTURE

After the agrarian reform, every Compi household suddenly had an additional twelve-man labor days per week (or more if one counts the time spent in the special services for the patrón) to spend at their own discretion. Some of this time was utilized for shorter weekdays and longer feasts and some for community meetings to discuss measures to hasten the expropriation process. Most time, however, was invested in more intensive agriculture and in marketing. Today, the main crop in Compi is no longer potatoes as it was during hacienda times, but onions, a crop which requires more care but also gives higher returns. It has a seven-month growth cycle and can be planted during most of the year on the irrigable valley bottom lands. It is grown for cash only.

The collapse of the hacienda system and the switch to onions as the main crop reduced the necessity for large families. A family was no longer obliged to furnish sufficient members to provide labor for the landlord as well as for their own needs. Further, the work required for onion raising is distributed over a longer period of time and can thus easily be handled by a small family. It is always possible to ask relatives for help for the remaining larger agricultural tasks, such as *oca* and potato harvesting. Thus couples now establish their own homes sooner after marriage. This fact, together with the increase of available cash and the security of owning the land one is cultivating, has led to a veritable building boom. Two-story houses with corrugated iron roofs and large windows, constructed with the help of local masons, are already more numerous than the traditional straw thatched huts which had only small windows or lacked them altogether. More and more bread, noodles, rice, sugar, and coffee are being purchased and the women have followed the men's example of wearing readymade clothing or having them made out of purchased cloth by one of the local tailors. Transistor radios are in general use and since 1967 even adolescent girls own bicycles. In Llamacachi, two men have saved enough to be able to afford to purchase trucks on an installment plan. Truck ownership is the most lofty ambition of most Compeños. This interest in transportation has resulted from the revolution in marketing on the altiplano since 1953.

Marketing

Since 1953, there have been drastic changes in the participation of the peasantry in the distribution and consumption of goods. The change has been from an incipient market economy, in which the Indian participated primarily on the village level with *mestizo* intermediaries, to a market system in which the Indian participates on both the village and the city levels.

In pre-reform times, marketing was based upon large transactions dominated by landholders and a few centralizing subsistence-oriented markets where the Indian traded with *mestizo* middlemen. In the first case, male heads of peasant households were responsible to an *apiri, a colono* in charge of the transportation of hacienda goods to the city storehouse of the landlord. The goods included regional staples plus animals, eggs and cheese. In La Paz, an *aljiri,* also a *colono,* sold the goods wholesale to *chola caceras,* (*mestizo* clients), Pazeños, and other landowners. Sometimes estate produce was sold directly to *mestizo* middlemen in the country.

In pre-reform days, there were fewer markets in La Paz, only one or two streets and a few patios open to vendors. Hacienda produce was brought on foot or mule back (later by truck) to the storage place in the houses of the landlords in La Paz, or to village fairs and the mines. Hacienda peasants could also sell their own produce in special patios reserved for them in the landlords' domain in the city. Peasants from free communities also sold in La Paz. Only *cholas* sold in the markets full time. Hacienda peasants traveled to La Paz only once or twice a year. Only *mestizos* were full time traders.

These large-scale transactions dominated by landholders existed in conjunction with a few centralizing subsistence-oriented markets where Compeños traded with *mestizo* middlemen. Peasant women from both free communities and haciendas bartered or sold small surplus staples such as potatoes, *ocas, habas,* barley, and for other staples and household needs: cloth, condiments, pots, soap, dyes, coca and fish. These peasants or *mestizo* traders in the country brought the produce back to La Paz. So on the local level, peasant women sold their meager surplus in Sunday fairs, in neighboring villages, in the plazas of provincial capitals or at the major feasts in the home community, that is, in Compi or San Pedro.

Today the picture is very different. As we have seen, in hacienda times, but more importantly, after the agrarian reform, Compeños migrated to La Paz on both a temporary and permanent basis. These migrants, usually women, began their marketing activities by bringing in produce to *tambos* (small marketing centers specializing in certain products), to daily markets or to a *feria franca* (a free weekly fair), where peasants sell their own weekly produce to the stall of a given market women or directly to the consumer. When in the city, they live with relatives and fictive kin or in quarters in the *tambos,* wholesale trading centers specializing in produce from a given area. These *tambos* are often the former patios of hacienda owners. After a certain length of time of temporary trading, these market women often decide to migrate permanently to the city. This decision does not, however, negate their ties with the country. They may continue to buy their merchandise directly from peasant producers either in the villages or in the city or from peasant or *mestizo* middlemen. Thus, for example, Marcela, who was born and lives in La Paz, sells altiplano produce, potatoes, *habas* and onions, brought in by her parents-in-law. Migrants also return to their communities of origin to sell and exchange food and sell manufactured articles directly to peasants at the weekly fair. Antonia is a case in point: She travels to the Yungas with vegetables every Thursday, which she exchanges for tropical fruits, oranges, bananas, and papaya. These she sells both in La Paz and in her home community on the altiplano near La Paz. Some migrants act as middlemen: Catalina sells woven cloth in La Paz which she buys on market days in her community of origin. Some migrants bring manufactured goods to the country fairs or work as chauffeurs or as assistants on trucks which transport articles to and from markets weekly. Formerly, in Compi, the *campesinos* or peasants did not sell the onions themselves in La Paz as they do today. In the beginning there were two middlemen, Mariano from Compi and Octavio from Llamacachi, who dealt in onions. They bought the crop before the harvest, per *c'uchus* or irrigation units, and harvested the crops themselves. The middlemen, in turn, loaded the onions onto trucks and sold them to *cholas* in the Rodriguez market in La Paz. Around 1947 there were only two trucks that regu-

Family group preparing onions for marketing in La Paz.

larly brought produce to La Paz, making only two trips per week. Today, eight trucks serve the community.

The relationships between producer, middlemen, vendor, and consumer is determined by *cacera* ties. These are reciprocal relationships whereby a person maintains a regular clientele by providing set service, better quality of merchandise at a cheaper price and/or credit. One's *cacera* ties and credit rating increases as one's social network expands. They often include both *paisanos* or countrymen as well as first, second and third generation migrants to the city. A more complete idea of this relationship may be gained if we describe Sofia's *caceras*. She is a migrant returned to Llamacachi from La Paz, but continues to sell her family's onions both in the free fair and in the market. "I have four good *caceras*. They are housewives. One day they sought me out in the street and so they became my clients. In order to satisfy my clientele, I give *yapitas* or 'little extras,' reserve good onions for them, and give them special attention and service. Sometimes I sell my goods at a lower price. So they search for me bringing sweets and their friends and relations so that they might get to know me and buy my wares. I myself am a *cacera*. I buy produce at home (in Llamacachi) in the fields. First I bought things at a higher price and so I became the favorite *cacera* of a number of peasants."

The *cacera* relationship is often based on credit. Many market women buy produce both in the field or at wholesale centers on credit and repay only when the produce has been sold. Credit is preferred only when the person has been a regular and reliable client. Sometimes these relationships are confirmed by written contracts. For instance, Isabel sells chickens in one of the large markets in La Paz. Yearly, she visits Cochabamba, where she was born, to file a contract with chicken, duck, and guinea pig raisers. She receives her produce on credit and returns her payment and orders for additional produce by letter. They then send the animals to her in a basket.

The market community is composed not only of a network of *cacera* relationships but also of a complex system of ranking which was inferred from informants' verbal ratings and by interaction.

Market women rank themselves verbally according to length of residence in La Paz which is revealed by fine distinctions—clothes and language. That is why Compi women pay particular attention to their attire when they go marketing and why parents are beginning to send their daughters to school so that they may speak Spanish and learn both measures and arithmetic. No one wants to be called a *moterosa*, a woman from the country who cannot speak Spanish. The fluidity of this ranking system becomes obvious when informants relate how a particular *moterosa* became a *de vestido*, a Western-dressed, Spanish-speaking, permanent city dweller, in one lifetime.

Association was not found to be a useful key to class position; persons of different rank sit side by side in the marketplace and participate in the same feasts and union meetings but the role a given person plays in a particular feast or union does parallel the verbal ratings discussed above, that is, a union leader is usually a *de vestido* or a *chola decente,* a city bred, Spanish-speaking, bejewelled and finely clad matron.

When in the city, market women not only change in their dress and speech but in their affiliations, one of the most important of which are those with the market unions which regulate the internal and external affairs of the market. Internally they act as courts of justice for disputant vendors; they control the distribution and inheritance of stalls in the streets or markets under their jurisdiction; defend their members against encroachment by nonmembers; arrange market feasts and occasionally contribute to the welfare of impoverished members. Recently they purchased land for new multistoried market buildings which are supposed to house the vendors as well as to provide office space for the union, a school, kindergarten, nursery, and infirmary with a full-time nurse in attendance.

Externally the syndicate mediates between the city government and the market vendors. It attempts to avert both police graft and unjust punishment of vendors. Before the formation of the syndicates, persons who could not pay rental fees for their stalls had been subject to the confiscation of produce worth more than the fee. Unjust fines for alleged failure to comply with the regulations governing the sanitary condition of their person and produce were common. For this reason a set fee has been established for the different kinds of vendors, for those with fixed stalls and for the ambulant ones. Syndicate leaders now actively intervene in their behalf and also arrange for the provision of additional areas for marketing. Finally, they communicate government requests for participation in processions on national holidays or rallies against communism as well as those of labor and mining unions for support in political manifestations.

The increase in and importance of marketing in the country is also reflected in the expansion of marketing facilities. Today, our altiplano vendor may sell in one of 11 major markets and 20 *tambos*, in addition to the adjacent streets. For example, in one particular market 368 regular stalls were occupied. At the same time, 280 vendors sold their wares in the adjacent street on weekends. When Compeños and other peasants come to town the market spills out onto the streets even more. These producer-vendors who sell in the street outside compete with the former *chola* vendors in the market. In order to deal with the situation, many regular market women have more than one place in which they sell, one within the market and one on the street (or in one of the three major areas opened to peasants on weekends). These "free fairs" were established during the first few years after the reform to decrease prices and promote direct producer-consumer exchange.

Compeños rent sites in the free markets or in a *tambo*. They used to sell in two free fairs but now they tend to sell in the environs of a large central market. When they migrate permanently they obtain a fixed stall or location, in or around the market. These stalls are prized possessions which are either inherited from mothers, acquired by joining a union, or obtained by purchase. A stall in the center of a large market costs about ten dollars. The stall is lost if it is not regularly used or union dues are not paid.

Compeños come to La Paz on Friday afternoon and return on Monday morning. Depending on the season, others arrive at the *tambos* for a four-to seven-day sojourn. They sell their own produce or that of kin or neighbors because this requires little capital investment. In her home community, the market woman buys

A La Paz market where some Compeños sell their onions.

the produce either by furrow[4] or load, with cash or on credit. Sometimes, in order to accumulate capital, she travels between the village and city. Capital can also be raised by borrowing from kin. In fact, many young girls begin their marketing activities with a small loan from mother, either money or produce. Once her social network expands and her credit facilities with it, she may graduate into selling products from other regions or products which require a greater capital investment. Returned migrants may also invest in a small store in the rural community.

At the same time, Compeños visit country fairs at least once a week. The fair in Jank'o Amaya shows a remarkable increase in both the quantity of foodstuffs from diverse regions of Bolivia and manufactured articles including consumer durable goods. Here one can buy fruits and coca from the Yungas as well as cloth and tools from La Paz. Today, as before, the agrarian reform peasants continue to sell and barter their surplus there.

Just as markets have grown in La Paz, so one notes a continuation and proliferation of weekly fairs in the rural areas. In the Department of La Paz an average of 16 fairs are held on any given day of the week.

---

[4] The produce from each trench in the earth made by a plow.

A Market Woman

Basilia, a 26-year-old market woman selling vegetables in a small street near a market may serve as a living example of the generalized pattern we have described above. Basilia was born in Compi and lives in La Paz with her aunt, the wife of her mother's brother. She came to La Paz before the reform when she was 12 years of age. She has been selling vegetables for 14 years, a trade which she learned "just like that" watching her aunt, her mother's sister, with whom she first came to the city to sell in a market. Basilia's parents and some of her siblings still live in Compi. One brother works in a store in La Paz. She visits and helps her family at harvest time and during San Pedro, Christmas and the school feast on May 25th. Her parents always send her some produce. She maintains close contact with Compi by dancing in a special dance group of migrants. She returns to her community of origin twice or three times a year.

Basilia's circle of social relationships now includes persons from many parts of Bolivia. Her friends come from La Paz, Cochabamba, and the altiplano. Just as her friendships span a wide area so do her business acquaintances. She buys her vegetables from peasant producers and middlemen from both the altiplano and the Cochabamba valley, situated 250 kilometers southeast of La Paz.

Basilia buys her produce once a week and earns approximately 80 cents a day. This is just enough to pay for her food.

Life in the market is plagued by many difficulties, both internal and external. Her neighbors are jealous of her profits and the police try to fine her. So, nine years ago she joined the union, not only to assure herself of a permanent location, but to protect herself from other vendors and the authorities.

Basilia's life history is informative in that it demonstrates three of the most important aspects of marketing: that marketing prepares the way for permanent migration to the city, that close ties between the city and country are maintained and that marketing is a means toward expanding one's social horizon.

3

Childhood

IN THIS CHAPTER WE SHALL DESCRIBE CHILDHOOD in Compi from the prenatal period through adolescence. We shall stress not only the physical development of the child but also his entrance into the community and the socio-economic role which he occupies there. Special attention will be placed upon his formal and informal education.

Compeños differentiate three distinct phases of childhood: *wawa* (infant), *yokalla* and *imilla* (male and female child), and *waynito* and *tawako* (male and female adolescent).

Pregnancy and Birth

Pregnancy is regarded as a natural occurrence which nonetheless demands certain precautions (see Chapter 7). The relationship between coitus and conception is fully understood but the actual physiology of sex is not. A woman who cannot, does not, or has never given birth is called a mule or a *machora* (man-woman); but both man and wife are considered culpable for sterility. The only means of birth control known are abortions which may be naturally or mechanically induced. The first category is procured by herbal potions concocted from eucalyptus leaves (*Eucalyptus globulus*), *payllcu* (*Chenopodium ambrosioidides*), *athipillu* (*Urtica magellanica,* both male and female plants) *sewenka* (*Cuperacaae carex*) and *sanu sanu* (*Alsophila* species) or by means of vaseline and cane alcohol. Abortions are said to be initiated mechanically by tying a belt tightly around the waist, carrying a heavy load, being beaten, and/or by energetic dancing. In spite of the frequency of abortions, family and community alike discourage these practices for they are associated with catastrophic hail (see Chapter 7).

The period of gestation is said to differ according to sex. Informants maintained that boys were born after 8 and a half to 10 months whereas girls arrived after 7–8 months. The average number of children born to a woman per family

School children.

is 5.35; they are spaced 2.05 years apart. Twenty-four percent of the total number of children a woman bears die. About half of these die under five years of age; about a quarter, under one year.

Both girls and boys are desired. A few weeks prior to birth the *usuiri* or midwife is requested to visit the home. These midwives are either men or women, some of whom are general magicians, whereas others, mainly women, specialize. They learn their trade by apprenticeships or by experience. Their services are remunerated and may cover the section, community, and neighboring localities. By reading the coca (*cf.* Chapter 7) the midwife predicts not only the sex of the child but the general outcome of the birth. On the second visit, four days prior to the expected day of birth, or when the birth pangs begin, the midwife examines the expectant mother to establish the position of the fetus.

Today all births take place in the home. However, during hacienda times children were sometimes born in the fields or in the hacienda house itself. The place of birth reflects changes in residence patterns. Previously, the young couple lived for a longer period with the husband's family before establishing their own residence, so most if not all children were born in the paternal grandparents' compound. Today first-born children may still frequently be born in that compound, but the others are born in the parental domicile.

The birth is attended by the husband, a midwife, the mother or mother-in-law, the mother's sisters and/or sisters-in-law. They warm the parturant mother by giving her a drink of coca, coffee, *kolipeke's* (*Rosmarinus officinalis*), *sanu sanu* (*Alsophila* sp.), *kantuta* (unidentified), chocolate or *k'ela* (*Lupinus angustifolius*). The midwife may attempt to turn the fetus by putting the patient on top of a blanket which is rocked back and forth, or by massaging her sides. During the actual birth she tightens the waistband so that the mother may deliver her infant lying down, kneeling, or sitting. After the birth the umbilical cord is severed with any sharp object available. Whereupon a drink of eucalyptus tea, *kolipek'e*, or *sanu sanu* is given to speed the expulsion of the placenta.

Immediately upon birth, the infant is sponged in warm water or urine by the attendant. Three to seven days after the birth the new mother bathes herself. On that day the birth is celebrated by inviting relatives living in the same community to a special meal prepared by a neighbor or female relative. This meal usually consists of meat or fish soup with potatoes, peas, and beans seasoned with oregano or wild thyme and *aji*, a red pepper (*Capsicum longum*). About the same time, adolescents and children stage a kind of nocturnal play, the *asuti*, to cheer the mother out of her melancholy. First adolescents play dice; then they mockingly slap the assembled adults for their marital misdemeanors, such as beating a spouse. After that, smaller children enter the room imitating various kinds of animal activities such as "mounting." Older actors then pretend to buy and sell the "animals." This is followed by a sketch about an old man and a woman who search for the Holy Cross represented by a boy with outstretched arms and a sack over his head. After blowing ashes representing incense into the boy's face, they act as though they wanted to dance for the audience. Later they fall asleep only to find that their child, a rag doll, has been stolen by the condor. Accusing each other of negligence and adultery they exit. The condor returns once more and is teased by the audience about his odor and the fact that he eats dead animals. Throughout the play all laugh as members of the audience take turns teasing the actors in the prescribed lewd manner and as the actors hit the audience for their impudence. The performance ends outside the house with a mock wedding while the relatives drink cane alcohol cut with water and chew coca until they fall asleep inside. This rite may be interpreted in a number of ways. On one level (which is what is expressed by informants) the *asuti* is a lewd play performed to amuse the parturant mother. On a symbolic level, the accepted decorous behavior between opposite sexes is licentiously flouted; the *normal* course of events is reversed, an old man and woman produce a child, and so on. These reversals, which are a common feature in Aymara rituals, will be analyzed in the chapters on religion.[1]

Unlike normal births described above, atypical or physically abnormal births result in a special series of events which demand magical treatment (*cf.* Chapter 7). Moreover, a child's birth may also be considered "socially abnormal," for example, incestuous or illegitimate. The term incest is applied to the following relationships: father or mother with offspring, siblings, first and second cousins, children of different mothers but the same father and vice versa, and ritual kin (*compadres*). Incest is considered "subhuman behavior" which occasions

---

[1] For a more detailed analysis of the *asuti* and a comparison with All Saints see p. 85.

want and sorrow. Illegitimate births do not evoke the same wrath, but when both sets of parents and the lovers forsake the child, the mother may resort to infanticide. Cases of infanticide were known to all. They occur in cases of infants born out of wedlock, incestuous unions and in large families. Although infanticide is decried, no special horror is attached to it unless the child is killed before it is named, for only then hail will fall. The child is killed by giving it alcohol or by smothering it with a blanket or with the mother's breasts.

Infancy

In normal cases, the infant is swaddled tightly with only the head left free, from birth to the fourth month. Compeños swaddle their infants to protect them from cold, to insure the growth of the limbs, to prevent the child from frightening itself and crying especially at night, and to provide tranquil sleep. After four months of age the infant is wrapped loosely in rags until he is one and a half years old.

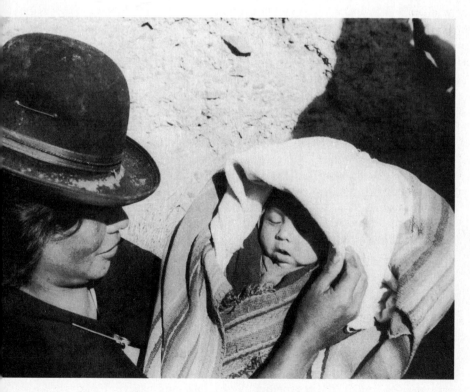

Mother and infant.

Infants are always breastfed.[2] Until the milk comes in, the newborn is given unfermented maize beer; then the infant is fed on demand for an average period of two years. Aymara mothers stress the importance of having "good breasts" to feed their infants. The child progresses from liquids to solids at eight months to a year, that is, from milk, juices, coffee, to premasticated and/or mashed bread, bananas, meat, *ocas*, potatoes, and *acu* (brown barley meal mush). At two years of age the child is weaned abruptly, especially if the mother is expecting another child. The child is weaned by applying the red juice of the berry *ñuñumaya* (*Soranum aurefolium Rusby*), *ají*, animal blood, or soot on the nipples, or by wrapping dirty wool around the breasts. Some mothers may even repel the child with a dead rat which they hold next to the breast each time the child attempts to breastfeed.

While birth, swaddling, lactation, and weaning mark the child's physical entrance into his community, baptism, the *rutucha*, or haircutting ceremony, and adoption signal the child's *social* entrance. He becomes a member of the religious community by baptism and a member of the political community by the inscription in the notary public's office. Names are chosen from the Catholic calendar (frequently the name appearing at the date of birth), and bestowed at baptism. In Compi, however, the *rutucha* is far more significant than baptism.

Baptism and/or inscription in the notary public's office and the *rutucha* are both normal ways of entering the community. Adoption is an atypical but by no means uncommon way of becoming a Compeño. Orphans, children of widowers or of remarried widows, and illegitimate children of relatives are adopted by older persons or childless couples for economic reasons and for the sake of company; for instance, adoption by grandparents is frequent because they need someone to help them with everyday chores.

The infant is considered an integral part of the community although it spend most of his waking hours in an *awayo*, or carrying shawl which is slung over both shoulders onto the back of the mother. Parents and siblings frequently fondle and play with infants. No infant is ever permitted to cry for very long. Mothers do try to prevent their children from crawling but a child is expected to sit at eight months, walk and give notice of its toilet needs at one to one and a half, and to speak "properly" at two.

Early infancy, known as "the dangerous years" is also plagued by illnesses such as whooping cough, diarrhoea, scarlet fever, bloody dysentery, grippe, tuberculosis, and *susto* or fright. These are ascribed both to natural causes, such as faulty care, and to supernatural ones. For example, fright is occasioned by seeing an apparition at night with the subsequent loss of soul. The treatment of these illnesses depends on the etiology of the disease: natural illness is treated by a variety of herbal teas whereas supernaturally-caused illness is magically treated (see Chapter 7).

The Child's Position in the Community

In the preceding paragraphs we have discussed the child's entrance and early development in the community. In the following pages we shall assess the

---

[2] However, some migrants in the city bottle feed their infants now.

Mother and children herding and doing homework by the lake.

child's role in the family and community. In hacienda times the child was involved in the three orders of kin ties discussed in the next chapter: the family compound, kin and nonkin who visited on special occasions, and distant relatives.

Today, the third sphere includes school friends and teachers as well.

Compi families expect their children to be quiet, hard-working, polite, humble, and controlled. Parents in turn are supposed to be loving, concerned, and protective. Parental love is shown by giving one's offspring food and nice clothes —preferably factory-made ones from La Paz. Parents teach their children the skills necessary for life in the community: girls learn agricultural tasks such as planting, weeding and harvesting, cooking, weaving, spinning, and marketing from their mothers. Fathers enlist the aid of their sons in working the fields, sewing by hand and by machine, knitting sweaters, and making nets. Formerly, boys also learned to weave certain articles which only men weave, for example, *bayeta* (sheep wool cloth woven on a European type of loom). They also fish along the shore with small hand nets.

By far the child's most important economic contribution to the family's income is herding. Children begin to herd by the age of four or five. Accompanied by older siblings, they first herd pigs and only after that are they entrusted with sheep. By the age of eight, both boys and girls go up to the hills about two hours away from the village to herd alone, and by the time they are ten, they are in charge of donkeys and cows. Cows and bulls are herded down by the lake where they eat reeds and lake weed.

Children rarely herd alone. When they are small they herd with their mothers, grandmothers, siblings, or cousins. Not infrequently they herd with a group of children of the same age who live in different sections of Compi. The following may represent a number of fairly typical instances.

One afternoon, one of us talked to Pablo, aged 15, who was herding cows by the lake about 15 minutes walk from the village. He was accompanied by his little sister Maxima, aged five. He said that he had been there all day since early morning; he left at about four because a storm threatened. About three to five minutes away his first cousin Pascual was herding cows, too. Both boys watched their animals silently, occasionally throwing stones into the lake to keep the animals from wandering off.

Contrasting sharply from these boys were three little girls, a girl of about 13 with her two cousins of about eight and nine who were herding pigs. The smallest girl scurried after the pigs constantly, stopping only from time to time to spin wool. The older two just chased after the pigs when they threatened to stray into the surrounding cultivated fields. These three played a kind of tag and hide and seek as they scampered around the field.

Mothers and grandmothers with children may also leave the house at 5 A.M. or a bit later to herd up in the hills. They take along their cooked lunch and return by 5:30 or 6 in the evening. Older children may go up to the hills also and some boys stay away for a week at a time taking turns herding with other relatives who have pooled their animals with their own family herd.

Whether herding is done in the fields near the village or up in the hills, it is still an isolating experience, for other herders may not even be at shouting distance, although larger groups of shepherds sometimes gather for lunch. In spite of this, all the children interviewed enjoyed herding. In general, herding in Compi is an activity which is adapted to the situational needs of the family, section and community. It is not strictly age-graded; for instance, when children are in school (or otherwise unavailable), men and women, both young and old, take over.

While herding is their major contribution to the economy, children six years and older also help to take care of younger siblings, in the fields, or with the cooking; even younger children carry water in jugs or tin cans from wells or the lake to their homes for household use, sometimes over considerable distances.

Common herding experience and similarity in age are two important considerations in the choice of a playmate. Playmates may be kin or nonkin, neighbors or children from another section of the community. Sometimes children arrange to herd with friends up in the hills, too. This seems to be a particularly common pattern for adolescent girls. But younger children meet and become friends by accident rather than by design.

Until the age of ten, boys and girls play together although a number of games are exclusively for one sex. Even though children do have friends of the opposite sex, their "best friends" are always those of the same sex. The type of toys one plays with is determined by sex too. Boys play with the yo-yo, cymbals, balls, marbles, tops, hoops and toy cars or trucks and a game called *chonta* in which they push a ball called *choncito*. Games for boys include two kinds of hopscotch, *tiwula* (fox) and *cumpu* (chick). Hopscotch was imported from La Paz in two forms, a "U" and an "L" shape, where it is played by girls rather than by boys. The former was brought to Compi about ten years ago; the latter is a recent introduction. Compi girls play with dolls, miniature clay bowls, and stones, and both boys and girls play tag.

Children of both sexes imitate adults in play. For instance, one day one of us saw a little girl of three digging a furrow with a toy hoe in perfect imitation of her mother who was working next to her. In another instance, a little boy and girl were imitating flute players in a fiesta by making the sounds and the appropriate gestures.

Imitation of adult activities is seen particularly when one watches little girls play with dolls. Some dolls may be played with all year round, but others, special ones, are taken out only on All Saints'. All these dolls have names. The little girls play with them, swaddling and wrapping them, "nursing" them, carrying them in their shawls, and dancing them up and down on their laps. (We also saw a small boy of two playing with a doll on All Saints'.)

Children of both sexes also romp with pet animals: puppies, kittens, lambs, piglets, and chicks. Teasing these pets is not uncommon. Little girls' favorite animals are those who are about to give birth to young, for these are nice playthings. Adults play with young animals too, especially with lambs which have lost their mothers.

In school both girls and boys are taught some dances. During school recess both play on the seesaw and slide (donated by the wife of a former president to many rural schools). Only the boys are taught soccer and gymnastics.

Aside from these, the only other sports enjoyed are swimming and fishing. Children of both sexes wade and splash in the river and in the shallow bay of the lake. Both sexes also swim, or rather dog paddle and dive under boats when the weather is warm enough. Only boys go fishing with nets, however. They fish for *karachis, k'ellus,* and other small fish in the rivers and on the lake shore. Sometimes they are permitted to tag along when their older brothers, fathers, or uncles go fishing out on the lake.

Certain taboos exist in play. As we have seen, some games and toys are sex-linked. In addition one may not play with strangers or in strange places. Furthermore, children are forbidden to be out playing after nightfall. One often finds children, especially boys, playing on the street from 5:30 P.M. after the animals have been put into their pens, but as the sun goes down, in go the children. Frequently children shun orphans for they possess few toys and have little food to share.

A favorite pastime in Compi is visiting kin or going to the store. Children are taken along on visits to kin (most frequently father's brothers), early in the morning before breakfast or for breakfast. The visits are to borrow tools, exchange gossip and news, and to discuss the crops. Children seem to enjoy these visits for then they can play with their cousins. They also enjoy listening in on adult conversation and jokes which they are not supposed to hear.

Children are often asked to go to one of the four tiny one-room stores to buy supplies such as a soft drink, matches, a candle, a handful of noodles, or a cup of sugar. These stores are the center of gossip where they can pick up choice tidbits of information.

Going along to market on Thursdays is also fun. A market is held in Jank'o

Playing marbles.

Amaya, 5 kilometers from Compi, every Thursday. Here one can buy staples as well as clothing and various utensils ranging from kerosene stoves to needles.

Children play a rather passive part in feasts except for All Saints' and the school feasts. They do, however, learn some dances either from each other, their parents, or the teacher. The dances which children are permitted to dance are the *Achachis, Cullawa, Llamero, Waca Waca,* and *Kusillo. Achachis* is a dance danced by small boys depicting old men or the souls of old men on All Saints'. We also saw it performed on Student's Day. *Cullawada* and *Llamerada* are danced with rented costumes, mostly by young married couples and adolescents. These two dances are the only ones in which there is an equal proportion of women and men. Children learn them in school and perform them in school feasts. Adolescents perform them during nocturnal dances in May and June as well. *Waca Waca* is an imitation of a bull fight which is acted by men, adolescent males and small boys on the feast of St. Peter. *Kusillo* is a comic dance performed by masked "clowns" on May 3d, the Feast of the Holy Cross. In contrast, the *Diablada* (the devil's dance) and the *Morenada,* (a dance representing Negroes) are reserved for mature men in Compi.

There are no formalized boys' gangs or girls' sets in Compi/Llamacachi, but we did discover gangs among the migrants in La Paz. During the Christmas season in the city, a band known as Villancicos, consisting of 12 boys and girls ranging from seven to 12 or 13 get together to serenade homes in the neighborhood. Members of the band are usually friends or kin who live in the same section of the city. The leader is often a bit older than the rest. They dress in colorful rags. Boys wear girls' clothes and vice versa. Some of them blacken their faces. All of them play some instrument—drums, flute, cymbals, or water whistles. They go from house to house to dance and play in front of the Christmas *crêche*. For their efforts they are rewarded with sweets, fruits, and/or money. This serenading continues from Christmas eve to the Feast of the Three Kings, on January 6th.

The general importance of children in the community may be seen in that most political assemblies dealt with school problems, and in that children play an active role in two important community feasts: on All Saints' and on Student Day.

Formal Education

Formal education is considered central in Compi-Llamacachi life. Four important leaders treat educational problems: the *presidente de la junta auxiliar*, the *presidente de la junta vecinal, alcaldes escolares,* and the secretary of education. The *presidente de la junta auxiliar* presides over the *presidentes de juntas vecinales* from the more important of the six zones, directs assemblies, and raises funds for the school in La Paz. The *presidente de la junta vecinal* is a liaison officer who relates the teachers' wishes to the peasants, welcomes visiting officials from La Paz, sends the *alcaldes escolares* to the capital to get the allotment of food from Caritas, a Roman Catholic charitable organization, and notifies parents when children miss classes. He also reports official matters, such as school attendance, to the director of the school district and is in charge of preparations for school celebrations. The most important of these occurs on May 25th, the anniversary of the founding of the school and on the September 21st Student's Day. Under the *presidente de la junta vecinal* are the secretaries of education and the *alcaldes escolares* of each section who take turns in supervising recess and in the preparation and distribution of Caritas milk for the school breakfast. In the smaller sections the secretary of education also assumes the functions of the *presidentes de juntas vecinales* and in one case even those of the highest sectional political authority.

The importance of education is not only reflected in the number of positions of leadership but also in the function of education in assemblies. Between November, 1964, and September, 1965, the school was the most important topic discussed in the assemblies. Topics discussed in assemblies included construction of school buildings, the preparation of school feasts, and the competence of teachers.

THE HISTORY OF THE SCHOOL

To gain some temporal perspective we would like to outline the history of the school in Compi and Llamacachi. Before the reform, the patrón in Compi prevented the establishment of a school and spared no effort to avert, sometimes unsuccessfully, the attempts on the part of Compeños to educate their children in schools outside the hacienda. In Llamacachi the situation was different. A few progressive Llamacacheños invited teachers to their homes to teach those interested. However, this early venture failed, for not only were the teachers unprepared, but they stayed for only very short periods of time. Some Llamacachi boys did, however, have a chance to gain an education in Hautajata, a community some 15 kilometers from Compi and the seat of the Canadian Baptist Mission. A few boys from Compi attended this school as well although their parents suffered harsh punishments from the patrón. In fact this caused a number of parents to migrate to La Paz.

In 1943, the Canadian Baptist Mission was able to build a primary school with three grades in Compi. But it was impossible for Compi and Llamacachi to build their own public primary school, a school with six grades, until 1958. Funds for this endeavor came from a number of sources: contributions from each household, the unused revenue of a cooperative, a Roman Catholic organization known as "The Schools of Christ," and Alliance for Progress.

The subject matter studied by the teachers is handed down to their pupils. Arithmetic, geometry, and most importantly civics are given priority over grammar, history, hygiene, and geography. Teaching is done by demonstration with charts and by letting children copy from the blackboard. Considerable attention is devoted to rote learning. Children are examined orally and in written form by outside examiners in the presence of their families. The regional director of education maintained that the most pressing problems in his area were the difficulty in convincing the peasants to send their daughters to school and the lack of cooperation on the part of the parents which resulted, in part, from community schisms.

School in Compi is not all work and no play. Two important feasts occur in the school year. Student's Day on September 21st and the celebration which marks the founding of the school.

Compi children gain knowledge not only in school and by the informal education of their parents in domestic skills, they also acquire specialized skills and knowledge of herbal cures, magical and religious rites, omens, the network of kinship and the local political structure and the traditional measurements of time, space, and weight, The extent of their knowledge of the foregoing depends on whether a member of the family is a specialist; the children of curers are better acquainted with herbal remedies than the other children in the community.

Stories

By gathering stories, drawings, and figurines we attempted to explore the child's imaginative world. A predominant number of the stories were told in Aymara by the father, male teacher, or grandfather. Most of them are animal tales followed by trickster tales, morality stories and tales of magic. Death, murder, trickery and fear of the strange are common themes. The animal tales deal with a whole range of beasts on land, air, or lake, from fleas to lions, eagles to ducks. The common domesticated animals play an unimportant role except for the dog and the donkey, but the fox, skunk, and condor are the most notable figures who even transform themselves into human beings. Another important character is the hummingbird, a supernatural who acts as an intermediary between man and the animal world. Human traits mark all these animals. Many marry humans. For instance, one typical tale is that of the Condor and the Hummingbird which goes something like this: The Condor takes a woman as his wife. One day the mother of the woman sees the Hummingbird in her garden destroying the plants. She tries to kill the Hummingbird, but the bird pleads for his life saying that he knows the whereabouts of her daughter. So the mother strikes a bargain: she will permit it to fly freely in her garden in exchange for information about her daughter. When the daughter returns to her family, the Condor kills the Hummingbird. This story possesses all the favorite elements in any Aymara tale: a love story between an animal and a human being, trickery, and death.

Pedro Ortemala and the Fox are the main characters in the trickster tales. Pedro Ortelmala tales are Spanish *mestizo* stories which deal with a clever man who always manages to fool ordinary persons, sometimes even the patrón. In one tale entitled *El Ortemala,* he tricks three sets of persons into giving him goods. Ortemala is always getting something for nothing but he never never gets caught.

In contrast to these fantasies, morality tales expound hard work, cooperation, self-abasement and nonaggression. One such story instills the moral that life is not all play. One day, a lazy little boy meets a dog and a bee on his way to school. When he asks them to play with him they refuse, for they have work to do: the dog has to help his master herd sheep and the bee says: "I am in a hurry; I am bringing a load to the hive. I shall be back immediately." The story ends with the statement: "José now understands that life is not a game. So he hastens to school, making the firm resolution to be like the diligent animals. From that day on he studies with joy and becomes the best pupil in the school."

Kindergarten. Generally the proportion of boys in other grades is much higher.

Magical tales involve place spirits, such as the *Chullpa* (grave or spirit of a pre-Incaic heathen) and a woman. This story tells of a young married woman whose husband is away. She is visited at night by a "man" just like her husband. When her real husband comes back they try to discover the identity of the stranger. In the quest, the husband and other men follow the stranger to a rock where they kill the stranger spirit and his mother by dynamiting it. This story illustrates another common theme, that of murder for revenge. Just as Condor killed Lorenzo (the Hummingbird), so the husband kills the spirit. The motive for murder, or the wish to kill is always revenge for harm done to some member of one's family, but it frequently happens that those who wish to avenge themselves die as well.

One such tale is about the Duck and the Fox. The Duck is in the lake. The Fox says to the Duck: "How is it that you have such beautiful offspring?" The Duck suggests that the Fox put its young into an oven so that they will become just as lovely as her own ducklings. The Fox does as he is told. His poor little ones get burnt to a crisp. Thereupon he tries to revenge himself but he cannot get at the Duck. In order to do so he drinks lake water to dry out the lake. The Fox dies in this attempt. His swollen belly bursts.

Fear of the strange is expressed in many tales. This is particularly true for the "Fox and the Chick" which stresses the danger of getting lost in a strange place. Others deal with the perils of the voyager and the herder who strays. A good example concerns a young girl who lives alone. A lizard falls in love with her and visits her in the form of a handsome youth. Thereupon the girl falls in love with him. One day, while herding sheep and expecting to meet her handsome youth, she is annoyed by an enormous lizard. She throws stones at him. Later, she discovers that the lover is the lizard. So she vows never again to speak to strangers.

Adolescent Girls

While childhood is subject to all manner of dangers, adolescence is the "time that brings tears to one's eyes." This period of life is idealized by adults, children and the adolescents themselves.

According to Compeños, adolescents (*tawako*, a young girl, *huayna*, young boy) are young unmarried persons anywhere from 13 to 19 or 20 years of age. Girls marry from the age of 13 to 22, but boys are usually a bit older, 20 to 25.

Adolescent girls do not participate in political assemblies, but they occupy a significant position in the socio-economic system. These girls, frequently, have no more than three years of schooling. Sometimes they attend evening adult classes. All of them help their families work the fields, herd, cook, spin, and take care of their younger siblings. Some weave as well, but their major contribution to the economic system is as onion vendors in La Paz. The following two cases are typical. Alicia, age 15, has gone to market in La Paz to sell her family's onions since she was ten. She travels on top of a crowded truck to La Paz with her aunt, her neighbor, and her girl friend, Lucha. They go into town once a week, on Friday, at least during the harvest. In La Paz, Alicia sells her onions at the market, acts as a go-between, and buys onions from Cochabamba to resell them in a local market. The money she earns must be handed over to her family, but sometimes she is given a small allowance for fruit or bread. While in the city, she stays over for a day or two at her aunt Elena's, her father's sister, who is a migrant to La Paz.

Raimunda, 21, sells onions too, but occasionally she takes along rabbits. Unlike Alicia, Raimunda acts as a "middle-man," buying onions in Llamacachi and Chua and selling these either to a central wholesale market or in the local market in La Paz. At least once a week, and not infrequently twice, she goes to town with a neighbor or, sometimes, alone. She also stays with kin in La Paz, in this case her mother's older sister, Daria. Since onions are the major cash crop in the two communities, the role of these adolescent girls is of immense importance. The economic well-being of their families depends on their skill in haggling and selling.

Adolescent girls also take part in the system of feasts in their own communities and in neighboring ones on the lake. For instance, it is customary to celebrate the feast of the Ascension in Sonkachi, some 10 kilometers from Compi and Pentecost in Jank'o Amaya. A family or a group of two or three friends will arrange to go to a feast together. These girls often go just to watch the dancers, but from time to time they are invited to participate, that is, to drink alcohol. They bring along their own cooked lunch which they eat with their families or with their friends near the plaza. Once in a while, 18 or 19-year-olds may drink a little alcohol, although it is frowned upon if young unmarried women imbibe.[3] Those who do drink are usually about 17 and are accompanied by their fiancés.

At the feast they meet the boys secretly; in fact, the usual pattern is that a boy and a girl decide to run away with each other at feasts, when their parents are inebriated. This is the most common way to enter marriage at the moment.

Adolescent girls go to Protestant services or occasionally to Mass. The Protestants attend church more frequently and regularly because a service is held every Sunday in Tauca and in Chua. The Catholics go to Mass very infrequently in La Paz and sometimes when Mass is held once a month in a neighboring community. There is no officiating Roman Catholic priest resident in the community although there are a number of lay Protestant preachers. Attendance at either service does not seem to be a meaningful experience whereas some Aymara rituals are, especially those carried out to fend off danger.

Adolescent Boys

Unlike the girls, some adolescent boys do attend political assemblies, but they do so only if their fathers are dead or if they need to represent the family interests. Marriage alone makes one an adult who may take active part in consultations and discussions.

These boys have an average of four years of schooling. Like the girls they, too, live in the family compound. They contribute by working in the fields, fishing, and herding. Some of them bring fish and/or onions to La Paz where female kin

---

[3] Married Aymara women are not supposed to get too intoxicated because they have to take care of their husbands who get very drunk.

or "middlemen" sell their produce. Not infrequently these boys have some work experience in La Paz, or, sometimes, in the Yungas. Through kin connections they may obtain a variety of jobs: chauffeurs, bakers, tailors, apprentices, or traffic policemen. These jobs are usually temporary, taken after they finish school and before they enter military service when 18 or 19. The following story told by Herman, an 18-year-old Llamacacheño, is very typical:

> I go to La Paz with trout. The trout and net are my father's but I also sell other people's trout. I have traveled to La Paz since I was ten; alone from the time I was fourteen. I go with onions, too. I have to give the money to my father. In La Paz I live with my brother or my sister. They have houses there. My father also has a house. I live there and my older brother lives there. My sister with whom I am very close, gives me food when I come. My brother gives me food—breakfast, everything—too. My father lives here. I travel alone and sell with my brother. I go in once a week on Fridays and return on Mondays. I take along potatoes, *oca*, *haba* beans and sometimes trout for my siblings. . . . I worked for the Ministry of Defense for a year. I was in charge of gasoline. My father and brother found me this job. My brother recommended me, he works as a chauffeur there. In 1964, after a year, I left and went into the army. Afterwards, I came back to Llamacachi, because there was no work there, in La Paz. Of course, if one has a profession, there is work. My father was here, so I used to come sometimes to help him. You see, my father is alone and has no one to help him. That is why I came back.

Adolescent boys attend and participate more fully in the fiesta system. They go farther away than the girls. Herman's social calendar may serve as an illustration. He goes to Chua, Lakachi, Huatajata, Sank'a Jawira, Huarina, Jank'o Amaya and Tiquina as well as attending all the feasts in Compi and Llamacachi. This means that he attends at least one if not more feasts a month. These feasts are two to three day affairs.

Herman goes with his best friends Lucho, Manuel and Ricardo, boys close to his own age, living in the same community. They drink heavily, each boy buying two bottles of beer or maize beer in turn. The drinking pattern is a mixture of the traditional Aymara one, in which men and women drink separately and the *mestizo* pattern learned in La Paz, in which men and women drink together. Previously, only married men of 25 or 26 were permitted to drink alcoholic beverages. Unmarried boys who came home drunk were beaten or given urine to drink.

Dances are the major form of recreation for adolescents. A married adult male usually organizes the dance group. He or someone else goes to rent the costumes in La Paz or Huarina. Weeks or months before the feast the group meets to practice. These groups vary in number from 10 to 30. They are always accompanied by musicians. The dances are the paired dances known as *Llamerada* and *Cullawada*. Partners may be related, but they need not be kin and are often just friends. These dances are performed on the major feasts: Saint Peter's (June 29th), Nativity of the Virgin (September 8th), Day of the Cross (May 3d) and Carnival.

Important rites in which a predominant number of adolescents participate are the *kachua, salvia,* and *asuti* (see Chapter 6).

For both girls and boys, visiting, both in the community and in La Paz, and going to markets are welcome breaks in the routine of life. Visiting for them as for others occurs in the early morning before breakfast. They also visit relatives and friends in La Paz. Girls make friends while selling onions in the market, boys, either while in the military service or on the job. These friends come from all parts of Bolivia. Some of them are Pazeños. On free Sundays the girls go to the movies, the zoo, to visit relatives, or for a *paseo*. A *paseo* is a ritualized promenade up and down a street for the express purpose of seeing people and being seen. They also go shopping for clothes. In La Paz, the boys get together with their friends, go to dances, and for a *paseo* or the movies for that is where the girls are. These rendezvous are secret.

One can also arrange to meet at one of the weekly markets in a neighboring community. Girls and boys meet there or on the road to the market by "accident." Vendors from La Paz and peasants from surrounding communities bring their produce to these markets. The market, however, serves not only as a place for the exchange of products, but for news and gossip as well.

In one of the alleys going off from the market plaza one can sometimes find older boys and young men gambling, known as "the game of rogues." Similarly on Sunday afternoons from 1 P.M. to 6 P.M., unmarried men and "adults" meet to play, on the soccer field or in one of the stores. They begin with 100 to 500 bolivianos (one to four cents). Some "spendthrifts" begin with 1000 (eight cents) or more. In an afternoon one can win or lose from 10 to 50 thousand bolivianos (80 cents to four dollars).

The other major male activity is soccer. Every year in each community a football club is organized and a secretary of sports elected. He is responsible for writing invitations to teams in other communities as far as La Paz to participate in the Easter matches. This official is also responsible for buying equipment, the uniforms and so on, from the revenue earned by leasing a parcel of cooperative land which is allotted to the team. The secretary of sports also organizes the practice sessions and safeguards the equipment. Formal matches are confined to the Easter week although informal soccer playing may also occur on Sunday afternoons, and, of course, in practice sessions for the Easter matches. School children play soccer the entire year.

Young Adulthood

No rite marks the adolescent girls' change of status but the occasion of a boy's entrance and completion of military service is considered most significant. Most boys of 18 or 19 go into the army for six months to a year.[4] The length of their sojourn depends on chance; lots are cast. "If they do not go the people talk, criticize, or scorn the boy." "They think that you are not a man."

The boys in Compi are stationed in a variety of places, for example, in La

---

[4] The military coup in November 1964 has considerably increased the number of persons drafted, so most Compeños who want to serve are able to do so.

Paz and Viacha. Here they meet others from all parts of Bolivia. For instance, Angel, a boy from Tauca was in a company with Tupizeños (persons from the south of Bolivia who are native Quechua speakers). These Tupizeños were all miners. The army also provides for additional education. They learn some military tactics and lore, civics, rudimentary Bolivian geography and history. When the boy returns from the army, he is feasted in his community.

Most of the boys who return to the community do not remain, however. Angel's comment with respect to his future is fairly typical: "I became accustomed to being in La Paz. It does not suit me any longer to remain here. Here one does not know what to do and I do not like to work in the fields. I want to find a job in La Paz."

Almost all of the adolescents questioned wanted to leave the community. The girls hoped to become vendors or domestics and the boys sought jobs as bakers, tailors, truck drivers, factory workers, and so on. Kin obligations require that at least the youngest son remain, but most of them complain that there was nothing "going on" in Compi.

> Here one has to work even on Sundays, and we do not have the chance to visit other places. Sundays are like any other day. In La Paz, on Sundays one goes for a *paseo*; others go to see a movie; still others go to see a soccer match. . . . My other brothers say that they do not want to return to work our father's land because they have become accustomed to life in La Paz. But I am the youngest and must remain.

The return from military service marks the beginning of periods of time when young men seek a likely spouse, for in spite of the prestige acquired by fulfilling his military obligations an unmarried man is considered to be an incomplete person. He cannot participate in community affairs nor assume any but the least important feast sponsorships. If he does not marry he may well retain the status of *yokalla*, or adolescent, for the rest of his life. Acquaintances are made while herding, on the market place, or during fiestas. During the latter occasion, he and his sweetheart may decide to elope. The boy may take his sweetheart to his parents' home or, more rarely, elope to La Paz for a few weeks. Elopement almost invariably arouses parental anger. For Aymara tradition presents a different marriage ideal according to which the parents make arrangements between themselves to marry off their children. Marriage by elopement is practiced by most present-day Compeños and was the rule in the past. Ill feelings do not last very long. The boy's parents break the news to the girl's parents bringing along coca and alcohol to appease their future in-laws. The latter must sooner or later give their consent to the union, for a girl who stays with a man only for a few nights is discriminated against and may find it difficult to find a husband. Usually, a period of trial marriage lasting anywhere from a few weeks to a few months follows the elopement until finally the couple's parents fix a date for the wedding and carry out the necessary preparations for the ritual which will give their children full adult status in the community.

The position a young man will have in the community depends on many factors. If he migrates to the city his connections with higher officials there and the extent he employs them to further the interests of the community will help him to establish his reputation. If he remains at home he must fulfill a series of ritual obligations and leadership positions to acquire higher status, or he may become a magician. If he speaks well at assemblies and knows fiesta rules to perfection this will also help enhance his prestige. Possession of land, a large house, or even a truck helps too, especially when combined with generosity in feast giving. Since it takes time for a person to fulfill his obligations to the community there is a strong positive correlation between age and prestige. In addition a man will be esteemed if he is not aggressive, follows rules of etiquette, or, when he is a magician, does not demand too much alcohol and food during magical ceremonies.

On the other hand a man may create resentment if he does not attend section meetings (as is the case with many Protestants), picks fights easily, uses violent means to protect his property, is remiss in returning borrowed money, refuses to pay quotas imposed on community members, steals, is suspected of black magic, indulges in gossip, and so on. Finally, although trial marriage may be terminated, a man will be criticized if he lives with too many women consecutively.

Some of the same factors will influence a young woman"s social position. A returned migrant may counsel women as to Western medicine, sewing, appropriate fiesta apparel, family quarrels, and the like. A woman acting as a curer, midwife, or diviner may enhance her prestige as well. She will be disliked for the same reasons as a man: black magic, stealing, gossiping, and an irascible personality being some of the disliked characteristics mentioned most frequently. Many of the means with which a Compeño enhances his position will be discussed in detail in subsequent chapters.

4

The Family

IN THE FIRST THREE CHAPTERS we have familiarized the reader with the general background of life in Compi as it unfolds through time and space. In the next two chapters we will present life in Compi in a more concrete manner, first by following a small number of Compi families through time and then by analyzing Compi politics as they are revealed in community meetings, squabbles over land and the life histories of key political figures.

It may already have become apparent to the reader that it is difficult to give a clearcut definition of the Compi family as a delimited unit. In a previous chapter we have mentioned how residence patterns changed when the agrarian reform and cash cropping rendered large work groups unnecessary and the city provided new possibilities for making a living. We have seen how, despite geographical distance, family ties are fostered between Compeños and their relatives who have migrated to La Paz. It becomes necessary then to seek a more flexible definition of the Compi family based not so much on a specific unit but on the changing network of ties which obtains between relatives. In order to accomplish this, we shall analyze those ties between an old man and his closer relatives from his birth to the present, comparing his case with other ones as we proceed. This man's life history illustrates most of the characteristics of a typical Compi household. This case shall also illustrate the set of relationships that constitute a household: the ties between persons who sleep and eat together in one of the clusters of two or four houses grouped around a small patio, which characterizes the Bolivian altiplano settlement pattern.

In the description of the familial relationships, four orders of ties may be discerned: one, ties between persons living in a compound and those who feel completely at home in the compound; two, those maintained with relatives and other persons who visit on special occasions such as birthdays, certain feasts and illness as well as ties based on mutual aid and migration; three, ties between distant relatives and four, *aini* bonds.

The first two kinds are frequent between the head of the compound and his married daughters and sons-in-law. But they may also exist between persons in the first category. In fact, the boundaries between the two types of ties are not very well defined in genealogical terms nor are the relationships strictly reciprocal. A son may visit his father's house and borrow anything he wishes without even having to ask, but his father may not necessarily be permitted to do the same thing in his son's home. Or, members of a large household may aid a cousin or uncle who has a small compound, and in return they may borrow anything from this relative, making themselves at home in his house.

Still, not all close relatives maintain the same ties. Siblings, or children who live in other sections of the community visit with less frequency. Even among close relatives living within the same sections there may be considerable differences.

A third set of ties is maintained between distant relatives. These assist occasionally, or visit at weddings or funerals. Neighbors, ritual kin, or *compadres*, other acquaintances and the secretary-general and *jilakata* in office also fall into this last group.

A final complex of ties, which is larger than the former but largely congruent with it, is that of the "guests" or *aini* who contribute money and food when one is sponsoring a fiesta. These *ainis* are repayable on the occasion when it is the *aini* sponsor's turn to hold a fiesta.

Manuel's Household

As a point of departure let us turn to the changing composition of Manuel's household over three generations which is illustrated below: Phase one of the domestic cycle is characterized by the dependence of the children on their parents, phase two begins with the marriage of one of the children, and phase three with the death of the original parents.

When Manuel was an infant he lived with his parents, his older brother Joaquin, and his two older sisters, Exalta and Justina, in one of three huts grouped around a patio. Later four or five other siblings were born of whom only Lino and Maria are living today. In a second hut lived Ambrosia, whom Manuel's father called "aunt," although Manuel is not certain about the actual relationship that linked her to the household. She remained a spinster her entire life. The third hut was used as a storeroom.

The composition of the household remained like this until Joaquin, the oldest brother, was married. He then brought his wife to live in the same hut with his parents and siblings for some nine years, during which time she had five children. First Francisco was born and when Francisco was about five, Bonifacio, a child of the same age, was adopted. No one knew from whence Bonifacio came originally. Francisco disliked him; thus it may not be surprising that he ran away at the age of nine. The man he escaped to took him to the valley of Sorata where—since the crops on the altiplano had failed that year—he exchanged the boy for food.

Manuel, when he was still almost a boy, married a woman much older than himself.[1] He moved immediately to the compound of his mother-in-law because she was a widow and had no other children and therefore needed somebody to help her both in her fields and with her obligations toward the hacienda. He slept and ate in the house of his mother-in-law, but his ties with his father's compound remained strong. He continued returning to his father's compound as though it were his own home. His father, in his turn, could come to Manuel's home to borrow anything he wished, even when nobody was at home.

Manuel's sisters set up their own homes, one in Compi and the other in La Paz (where she married a man who was from Capilaya originally), but Lino, the youngest brother, remained in his father's house which he inherited (following general Aymara practice) at the death of his father.

We have depicted, then, a basic set of ties between a father, his sons and daughters, the wives of his sons and their children, and a number of other persons who either cannot establish a home of their own or are necessary to complete or replace ties which are either deficient or which have been severed. An example of the first situation is the "aunt" of the father of Manuel, who had no place to go because she was unmarried. The tie between her and Manuel's compound may well be a carry-over from sibling ties which normally would have been altered through marriage. She may also have become included in the family by intensifying a relationship of mutual aid, a custom which we shall explain later. Both cases are frequent in Compi. Alternatively, if all the children have established their own homes, if even the youngest son (or the son who marries last) has not remained at home, or when there are only daughters in the family, then the parent-child relationship may be re-established either by adopting a child—frequently a grandson or granddaughter—or by asking a son-in-law to establish uxorilocal residence.

The second category of ties, those based on mutual aid, may be seen in that two of Manuel's sons frequently assist Joaquin and Lino, Manuel's brothers, and Joaquin in return treats Manuel's sons as though they were his own children.

Furthermore, Manuel receives help from his daughters, and his son-in-law, Faustino, never fails to pay a visit when someone in Manuel's compound falls ill; but Mario, one of Manuel's sons, rarely lends a helping hand. Similarly, Joaquin is aided by all his daughters and one of his sons, but the other son keeps aloof because his wife does not get along with her father-in-law.

Land Tenure and Inheritance

But the order of importance in these ties, especially of the first and second types, is manifest most significantly in land tenure. We have indicated that land tenure depended only partly on the will of the patrón, although there were other

---

[1] This type of marriage is rare in the community. It is practiced sometimes for economic reasons. A poor young man may marry into a family where there are only daughters, establishing matrilocal residence and later inheriting the land. The advantage for the wife's family is the fact that a poor man is always ready to move to his wife's home, furnishing invaluable aid in agriculture, while a rich son-in-law may well refuse.

arrangements between peasants of which the patrón had little awareness. Let us turn again to Manuel's family to illustrate how the various ties within the compound are reflected in land allotment.

The "aunt" who lived in Manuel's compound received *chiquiñas*, a few furrows of land, in each plot, from Manuel's father. She acquired these in return for assisting Manuel's father and could dispose of the produce from them as she pleased. When Manuel went to live with his mother-in-law he took possession of the whole parcel of land but he gave his mother-in-law the right to the produce from a certain number of *chiquiñas* in the jointly cultivated plots. She however, contrary to Manuel's "aunt," took little if any advantage of the degree of independence this could have given her, and continued to have her meals with her son-in-law. Manuel in turn received some four to six furrows in every one of his father's parcels, in return for helping his father. He acquired his father's land completely when his siblings were in La Paz for a few years. After the death of Manuel's father, his youngest son Lino gave his mother *chiquiñas* from the third part of his father's *sayaña*, which had been allotted to him provisionally, but like Manuel's mother-in-law, she continued to have her meals with Lino. After Manuel's siblings had come back from La Paz, his father's land was divided permanently among the three sons.

If a man possesses sufficient land, he consigns *chiquiñas* in each plot he owns to his married daughters. At his death his oldest son, who assumes the paternal functions, continues the practice. The daughters or sisters are expected to aid their father or oldest brother in return for the *chiquiñas*. If they do not appear for work occasionally, their annual allotment of land is discontinued. Thus, in spite of national laws, men and women do not inherit equal shares, at least not in Compi and Llamacachi.

Nevertheless, especially during hacienda times, the fact that a woman could count on the usufruct of a few furrows of land had considerable importance. In difficult times, a woman from Llamacachi or from one of the *comunario* families in Compi who had married a *colono* could always return with her husband to her own family, remaining there until the situation had improved. In this way Amasi, a part of Compi proper, almost became depopulated. Its inhabitants married *comunarias* from neighboring Tauca, continuing to live there even after they had resumed working for the hacienda.

The allotment of usufruct rights, and especially the definite distribution of land, becomes more complex when *utawawas* (adopted children or landless families living on the land of richer ones) and/or illegitimate children inhabit the compound, because their rights are much less defined than those of legitimate children. In fact, both in Compi and in Llamacachi, such situations cause frequent disputes within a family.

Pedro is a good example of an *utawawa* who had to struggle in order not to be disinherited. He lived with his grandfather from the age of 16 until the old man's death which occurred when Pedro was away in the military service. At first his grandmother continued living with Pedro's wife, but soon Pedro's father's youngest brother insisted on taking the grandmother to his house, probably with the idea that Pedro's part of the land would then pass to him. It was only through the intervention of the secretary-general in the Council for Agrarian Reform in La Paz, that this scheme was blocked, if only in part, and that Pedro did not lose all his land.

In some cases, illegitimate children may not be able to inherit at all. For an example of this situation we shall return to a branch of Manuel's extended family. When Pascual (Manuel's brother's son) returned from La Paz, his father's father's sister gave him half of her parcel of land. She did this in order that the grandchildren of their *utawawa* would be deprived of their inheritance. The *utawawa* had come to their home from another community, along with one child who in turn had illegitimate children. These showed a striking resemblance to the adopting father of their grandmother and so Pascual's great-aunt wanted to thwart the rights of children born in such an ignominious manner. In effect, when the great-aunt's husband died, Pascual refused to recognize their rights.

The system of inheritance and land distribution in general was very similar in Compi and Llamacachi, although the patrón's intervention in Compi did produce some differences in the two communities. But the patrón intervened only when the system ceased to function properly, for example, when a person accumulated so much land that his family was not able to fulfill all the obligations pertaining to the usufruct of each parcel. In this case an overburdened family would have to cede their rights to some of the parcels to other persons. Sometimes this forced redistribution was conducted by the patrón. Nevertheless, a family could often cede the surplus parcels directly to a person of their own choice, frequently one within the holder's own extended family. Thus Pascual and his father were able to amass usufruct rights over four different *sayañas*.

While in Compi *sayañas* did thus change hands within and outside of the extended family, land in Llamacachi tended to remain within the same family, with the exception of those families who had lent land to poorer ones in return for their labor. Such original *utawawas* frequently became the legitimate owners of the parcels they had received. On the whole, however, land tenure patterns in Compi were very similar to those in Llamacachi.

Changes in Households

As we have mentioned earlier, the households became smaller after the agrarian reform. This process of individualization can be made vivid if we return to Manuel's family to analyze the changes which have occurred in the present generation. Tomasa was the first of Manuel's daughters to marry. She went to live with her husband and his parents, first in common-law marriage and then in formal marriage. Then, in 1955, Mario, a son, brought his future wife to his father's house. He constructed his own temporary home even before his formal marriage, when he was still only joined to his wife in common-law marriage because, as he says, there was not enough room in his father's patio to raise his own chickens; his eggs could become mixed up with those of his father's chickens. The main objection his parents had to his move was that the community might think that they had thrown him out of the house. He continued to eat at his parent's house, however, because he and his young wife had neither kerosene stoves nor cooking utensils. Nonetheless, the onions which Mario had planted in the plots set aside for him by his father were ready to be harvested, so he could soon purchase what he needed in order to move to his new home permanently. Six years later when he had earned enough money from the sale of onions, he was finally able to build a "proper" house, with a *calamina* (corrugated tin) roof.

At this time Manuel and his two younger sons were living in two houses at the same time. In the meantime Tomasa's husband had died and her parents decided to keep her company. Since their old house could not be left unattended, part of the family slept there. Thus, when Pedro got married in 1961, he continued to live and eat in his father's old house as before. But after a few days he and his wife grew weary of walking from one house to the other at night. When Pedro and his young wife began arriving late for dinner, Manuel became angry and told them to cook at a separate hearth. Three years later Pedro decided to build his own house. He felt that having his own house was more prestigious than living in his father's house. After all, if his brother Mario and many other young men had been able to build houses, why could he not do likewise? Until a year before he built his house, he had merely taken food out of his father's storehouse, but now he asked his father for separate parcels of land where, like Mario, he planted onions to pay for his construction materials. From that time on he also stored his own produce separately.

It becomes evident that both Mario and Pedro ceased living and eating at their parents' compounds much earlier than the previous generation had. Manuel can scarcely be considered as an exception because going to live with one's mother-in-law when male helpers are scarce in her family was an old, established Aymara pattern. Nor did either Mario or Pedro have any urgent reason for establishing their own compounds so early. They were merely following a general trend.

However, let us not give the false impression that changes in the Compi family have been revolutionary in nature. Sons continue to help their fathers and only at their father's death is land distributed permanently among the children. Thus they are not completely independent until the father's death. Moreover one of the sons, usually the youngest or the one who marries last, normally continues to remain in his parents' home, or, if he does not, he has the obligation of caring for his mother until her death.

Effects of Migration

Changes in the Compi family both in the past and the present are strongly influenced by migration to La Paz and to the Yungas. Let us turn again to the family whose history we have used previously to illustrate the effect of migration. Life was becoming increasingly difficult for Joaquin, Manuel's older brother. During the year he was *jilakata* he had permitted his relatives from Llamacachi to channel the water from the irrigation ditch to their fields once and as a result he had been punished by the patrón. Also, his oldest son, Paz, was going to school in Huatajata, a fact which displeased the patrón very much indeed. So, in 1941, for these reasons and because of the ever-increasing work load, Joaquin began to plan his leavetaking for La Paz.

As a first step, he purchased land on the outskirts of La Paz. Then he sold the crops he had produced in that year. Finally, one night in 1942, he purposely burned the roof of his house and left with his entire family. Since he had not yet constructed a house on the plot he had purchased in La Paz, he rented a room in the house of a nearby peasant (for at that time this zone, which is now completely urbanized, was still to a large extent occupied by haciendas). Assisted by his *compadre* who had come to La Paz a few years earlier and who worked for a large bakery at the time, Joaquin soon found a job distributing bread for the same bakery. The whole family helped with the bread distribution, a job which he continued until the end of his sojourn in La Paz.

Joaquin's youngest brother Lino, his sister Maria, and his mother, decided to leave the hacienda, and to construct a house on Joaquin's property. Lino and Maria also distributed bread from the same bakery, while their mother contented herself with selling popcorn near their home.

Since distributing bread could be done early in the morning until eight o'clock, both brothers searched for a job to occupy the rest of the day. Joaquin found a job in a hardware store and Lino a position in an import company by the good graces of Faustino Gonzales, who came from Capilaya originally. As a result of the friendship between Lino and Faustino Gonzales, Lino's sister, Maria, soon married Faustino. Finally, the two daughters of Joaquin, who had been helping with adobe making, landed jobs as servants.

Joaquin in turn helped other relatives. His godchild asked him if he could build a house on his plot. He forthwith granted him this favor without demanding anything in return. After all, his godchild had once saved his life when he was ill in the Yungas.

The importance of kinship ties and ties with other members of the community or origin with respect to migration continues to the present. Joaquin's son, Paz, found a job after the agrarian reform through the political influence of his Compeño friend, Fausto.

Migration in Llamacachi is of a somewhat different nature than in Compi. Previous to the agrarian reform, there was very little emigration to La Paz, and only a few families migrated because of land shortages. But in this generation, the situation has changed. The combination of increasing population pressure and more possibilities open to the peasant has induced young men and women to leave for La Paz. Migration seems to be a gradual process in Llamacachi. Many young men have built houses in La Paz where they stay when coming to La Paz to sell onions. The idea is that their children will later live in the houses permanently.

Most of the migrants from Compi and Llamacachi own their own houses. The rest rent a room or two in the homes of relatives or elsewhere. As a corollary, many Compeños let rooms to relatives or to strangers. Many close relatives are also permitted to live free of charge.

One might expect the migrant families in La Paz to be smaller and less cohesive than their Compi and Llamacachi counterparts, but the contrary appears to be true, at least regarding the size of the families. Fathers purchase land on which their sons later construct houses also. Moreover, relatives are taken in as renters; young Compeños in search of jobs or secondary education find a haven among close relatives and others even work for their relatives, learning their trade from them. Sometimes the household includes *compadres* and other acquaintances from Compi and Llamacachi. Furthermore, in many cases, there is a constant coming and going of close relatives who come to sell onions in La Paz or who have come to work in La Paz on a temporary basis. In addition, many migrant families have economic interests in Compi and Llamacachi, that is, they own land there or are entitled to produce from land. Therefore, many return to their home community for a few days or for a few weeks during the harvest and sometimes during other periods of intense agricultural activities. While the migrants are in La Paz, some relative takes care of their land or sometimes their wives live in the country most of the time and take care of the fields. Those who do not have any economic interests in Compi at least visit their families during fiestas, weddings, or other important events. Thus the majority of the migrants are far from cut off from their extended families.

Agustin, for instance, who migrated to La Paz in 1944, still receives produce from his relatives in Capilaya. He continues to have access to some three or four furrows of land in each plot which are being cultivated for him by his brother and his brother-in-law. Moreover, he purchased a small plot of land from the former patrón which his brother-in-law cultivates for him. While he receives only half of the produce from his allotted furrows, he obtains the entire harvest from his purchased plot. To compensate his relatives, Agustin sends goods which are not produced in Compi to his brother and his brother-in-law two or three times a year. He himself usually comes to Capilaya only during fiestas, thus his share is sent or brought to La Paz when one of his relatives goes to sell onions. When vacations do permit a longer stay in Capilaya, he aids his relatives and in return simply receives board. He lives in his own house which is cared for by his nephew whom he has allowed to live there.

Francisco has a similar arrangement with his migrant son, Geronimo. In addition to giving his son a few furrows of land, Francisco lent him money which he never expects to be returned. At the same time, Geronimo helped his younger brother enter military service advancing him money and a trunk. Geronimo's influence on his father is so great that he has succeeded in converting him to Protestantism and to abstinence from alcohol. "One enters easily into quarrels," he had told his father, "and if someone should beat you because you insulted him while you were drunk, this would make me very sad."

Exceptionally strong ties exist between Compeños and Llamacacheños whose sisters or daughters have migrated to La Paz to deal in onions. These women market the onions of their parents and siblings, thus remaining in constant contact with the rest of the family.

Finally, many school children visit their grandparents in the country during school vacations, and thus do not become completely estranged from life in the country.

In some cases, however, tensions result between migrants and their families at home because of claims on land made by siblings or other close relatives in

La Paz. Lino, for instance, has been cultivating his brother Emeterio's share of land on a sharecropping basis for many years. Emeterio rarely comes to Compi and so Lino is contriving to take the land away from his brother. Like many migrants, Emeterio has changed his second name to make it sound more Spanish. Since Emeterio's land titles are all in his former name, Lino calculates that it would be difficult for Emeterio to win a case in court. Other Compeño migrants we have interviewed complained bitterly that their relatives in Compi pretended not to recognize them when they visited their home community because they were afraid they might have to share their plots. Such disputes are rare, however, for male members of Compi families who have migrated to La Paz have a very limited claim to land at home. Like married women who have remained in the community, they are allotted a few furrows of land in each of their father's or eldest brother's plots of land; this is kept only if they reciprocate with gifts or labor or both. An exception to this rule occurs when the land had been divided before a person has migrated. Other influences of returned migrants on the community shall be treated in the next chapter.

More Distant Ties

We have seen the complex interweaving of the first and second order of ties reflected in changing composition of a compound in different periods of the domestic cycle, in land tenure, and in migration. In the following pages we shall address ourselves to the third and fourth order of ties based on visits of distant kin, ritual kinships, and "guests" or ainis.

We shall illustrate the third order of ties by describing the day of the compadre in Manuel's compound. This feast commemorates the role of the godparents of the wedding. On a pre-established date once a year, Teodoro, Manuel's "godchild of wedding" visits his wedding godparents accompanied by a small retinue consisting of his father, brother and five other persons. The padrino, Manuel, is accompanied by his brothers, sisters, nephews, cousins, some distant relatives related to his wife and some male in-laws of his niece. They exchange food, coca and alcohol which are always served in twos, probably to symbolize the marriage bond. These more distant relatives, second cousins and so on, are also important members of the retinue at other family or life crises, feasts, baptisms, the rutucha or haircutting ceremony, the feast which ends the young adolescent male's military service, weddings, birthdays and funerals. They also often visit community fiestas.

At this point, it becomes necessary to write a few words about ritual kinship or compadrazgo.

Compadrazgo is an extremely widespread means of establishing relationships between unrelated persons or strengthening bonds between related ones. Although compadrazgo is a Spanish term for a custom widespread in Europe as well, a variety of similar practices were present in Precolumbian lowland and highland, Mesoamerica and South America. Compradazgo ties are established most frequently at baptism and marriage. In the former case, a bond is created between the parents of the child and a couple who fulfill a number of ritual and economic obligations during baptism. Reciprocal obligations between the two couples may continue for their entire lifetime, in most cases regardless of whether the god-child remains alive or not. These obligations are often supplemented by ritual prohibitions such as taboos on intercourse and marriage between *compadres*. More-over, the reciprocal obligations may be extended to relatives of both parties, creat-ing a network of potential ties which may be activated when the need arises.

In the case of marriage, *compadrazgo* ties are established between the par-ents of the newly married couple and the godparents as well as between the latter and the godchildren.

Compadrazgo-like ties may also be established in a variety of other con-texts. Thus a person may be asked to be the *compadre*, or sponsor, of a child's first communion ceremony, or a club's party. Such acts may or may not create lasting ties.

Compadrazgo ties may be established with persons from the same or dif-ferent locality, from the same or different social class. If *compadres* are not of the same social class the obligations are not of the same nature. For instance, individuals of a lower class seek godfathers among higher placed ones in order to create patron-age links, which may give them access to higher placed governmental authorities, credit, or other scarce "goods." In return they may offer small gifts of produce or provide menial services. *Compadrazgo* networks vary greatly in importance. In some South American societies such as in Moche (Gillin 1945) they are a major means of social intercourse. In Compi they are merely a supplement and/or re-inforcement of already established ties based on kinship, being neighbors, friend-ship, and other less structured relationships.

In Compi and Llamacachi this is the institution that ties the parents and godparents of a child at baptism and/or the *rutucha*, and the godparents of a mar-riage with the newlyweds. These *compadres* are always a married couple. The same couple usually take upon themselves the duties and obligations of both a baptism and/or *rutucha* and a wedding. These *padrinos de matrimonio* (godparents of the wedding) are chosen as the godparents of the first child, either son or daugh-ter, born to the young couple too.

Godparents are neighbors in the same section of the community, friends and/or relatives. If they are kin, they are usually distant consanguineal or affinal relatives. When one's choice is a person from the same section, as is frequently the case, one usually chooses persons who are in a similar economic situation so that the economic duties such as gifts and labor exchange between persons aligned by *compadrazgo* are of equal value.

Compadres are often friends with whom one has worked or feasted. For example, Dámaso sells sheep in the Yungas. He met his *compadre* when a person from a neighboring section sold the *compadre* a mule. But the family of his *compadre* in the Yungas was already known since he lived in an area in the tropics which had belonged to the owner of Chua, the neighboring altiplano community. In fact, Dámaso's father used to trade in the area of the Yungas prior to the reform. Dámaso himself carries along altiplano vegetables to his *compadre*. He often stays a week and helps him harvest coca and dry and shell coffee. Similarly, Faustino has three *compadres* with whom he has played in the same band. Young women who market together often reinforce friendship by establishing *compadrazgo* ties. Persons are also chosen to fulfill the role of ritual kin if one has already established a pattern of reciprocal work exchange (*aini*) or of companionate drinking. Thus, *compadrazgo* in Compi tends only to reaffirm former ties based on common work experience, friendship and/or kinship rather than to create new ones.

These persons are frequently neighbors but it is not uncommon that they live in La Paz and the Yungas Valleys. The advantage of choosing a neighbor is that one is familiar with his reputation, that is, whether or not he is a generous godparent who gives rich feasts. The disadvantage is that one may be called upon to help one's godparents, especially during harvest. Thus a few Compeños prefer to establish ritual kin ties outside the community, and a few Compeños have *compadres* in higher social positions, such as lawyers, sons of the former landowner, and so on. *Compradrazgo* bonds between those of unequal social status are often nothing more than tenuous ties based on occasional visits unless they are associated with professional interests as well.

In La Paz, the *padrinos* are supposed to present their godchild with a new set of clothes at baptism and to pay for the baptismal fee. In Compi, one celebrates the *rutucha* or first haircut. At this time, godparents are required to give the child a feast at their own home. Besides playing host and master of ceremony, their retinue or *aini* provide the largest part of the food and a servant who serves the guests which include not only their own relatives and *aini*, but also those of the parents accompanied by their followers. They also provide coca, alcohol, money and a set of clothes.

Godparents of the wedding are chosen by the wife's parents. On the day of the wedding, they accompany the young pair to the *cantón* seat for the civil wedding. There, they pay the notary public's fee and provide for a drink of alcohol to celebate the occasion. Upon their return to the community the godparents invite the newlyweds for a meal and provide them with their wedding apparel. The godfather also contracts a brass band. Both godparents play an important role in the wedding proceedings and also after the wedding, for the godfather is supposed to arbitrate familial quarrels. Divorces are often blamed on the godfather's negligence in his role as peace maker.

Other than these three occasions: the day of the *compadre* described on page 46, the *rutucha*, and the wedding, ritual kin visit each other when they are in each other's vicinity, and drink with each other on feast days. The child's parents also aid the godparents in agricultural tasks during the sowing or harvest and in return give their godchildren some of the produce. When the relationship is a close one *compadres* also help in the preparation of feasts, such as *Todos Santos* (All Saints').

We have observed that *compadrazgo* is not necessarily a relationship with great importance. Within the third order of relationships we have been discussing, the *aini* relationship plays a more central economic role. The *aini* relationship is based on either labor exchange and/or financial assistance and presence at feasts. Labor exchange is less important than a relationship based on *minga*, labor exchanged for produce. One's *ainis* might be relatives, persons who are trying to establish themselves in the hierarchy of feast sponsorships, friends, acquaintances, *compadres,* neighbors, and/or members in a particular section. The bond is merely one of financial support which is severed once the money is returned in a feast given by the initial lender.

Common interest and experiences are the foundation for friendships. Informants often mention cousins as good friends—many are persons of the same age and sex with whom the individual herded together as a child, with whom he went on marketing trips, worked in neighboring fields, attended the same religious services or feasts, played football or panpipes, belonged to the same class at school or military service. These activities bring Compeños into close and continued contact with persons from many communities, cities, and regions of Bolivia.

"One of my best friends is Nimesio," claimed Kassa, "we have known each other since we were youngsters herding up in the hills. We still go to Tiquina, a community about one-half hour away, for visits. Now I am even more intimate with him because he married a cousin of mine." Kassa has another friend near Copacabana, whom he met when trading animals. He stays over at his home and eats with him although he trades with others in the community as well. He numbers Prudencio and Teodoro, both cousins, among his friends, and he goes to visit them when he needs assistance in the fields or money. On Sundays he accompanies them to Protestant services. There he meets his other friends. One of his best friends with whom he herded and molded clay figurines, as a child, is now in La Paz working in an aluminum factory. Since the friend owns his own house in La Paz, Kassa stays with him on his trips to town.

Kassa's list of friends is typical in that most are formed as a result of economic or religio-festive activities experienced together, herding and marketing, or common attendance at a religious service. Among Catholics, friendships are formed at feasts. Most men mention that those with whom they drink at feasts both at home and in neighboring communities become friends.

Military service and working experience, as a domestic or in the market, often leads to friendships which are kept alive by the fact that Compeños travel widely for economic and social reasons.

In the preceeding chapter we have stressed both kin and nonkin social relationships. The dynamics of these will become even more apparent when they are described again within the context of Compi politics, feasts and religion.

5

The Community

T HE DIFFICULTY OF DEFINING THE COMPI FAMILY extends to the community as a whole. In part this is due to one of the same reasons which makes it difficult to define the family. The community may be considered as extending itself to La Paz to include the migrants who have continued to exercise a strong influence on their birthplace. In part, however, this is also due to the complex relationships between different sections (semi-autonomous parts) of the community, whose origin we have already described in the first chapter.

As we have stated, each section is separated from neighboring sections by hills. They have formal boundaries within which lie most of the plots of land of the component households. Politically, sections form separate entities in the sense that each has a set of authorities and that most political councils take place on meeting grounds in the center of each section household cluster. From our analysis of Compi history it became clear that the degree of autonomy and the alliances between sections has constantly changed throughout Compi's history. As we shall see, these ties are still changing at present. Thus, in hacienda times the common obligations created bonds among all Compeños. Some sections were subordinate to others because they did not have a complete set of local authorities. Today intersectional ties are looser and mainly concern the school, the church and fiestas. Marriage ties crosscutting sections have remained the main bond between sections but, because a high percentage of marriages take place within the section, kin ties have also contributed to the maintenance of section identity.

Intercommunity politics are even more fluid than intersectional politics. Pre-reform counties representing the lowest rung in the national administration were larger but had effective control over free communities in their jurisdiction only, while haciendas were largely autonomous politically. Today counties have proliferated, centering in newly established nucleated peasant villages. Modern county jurisdiction extends over both free communities and former haciendas. Furthermore, today, county administration is but one among many means by which a peasant is politically linked with the nation. After the agrarian reform, an independent political system patterned on labor unions was established by which hacienda peasants could govern themselves on the local level and have a voice in national politics through the subregional, regional and departmental organs. Finally, a special Ministry of Peasant Affairs and a Council for Agrarian Reform was established in the capital itself where peasants can make petitions either through the two aforementioned channels or by going to La Paz themselves.

In this chapter we shall analyze network regularities which underlie section, community, and regional (county) organization and their relationship with the national government.

Intersectional Ties and Disputes

Our main reason for treating Llamacachi and Compi as a single community is the fact that there is considerable intermarriage between them while marriages with neighboring communities, except for those with adjacent sections of such communities, are infrequent.

Marriage within a section averages 56 percent, marriages between sections 32.5 percent, and marriages outside the community average only 11.5 percent.

In hacienda times, working together in the fields of the patrón must have contributed to section intermarriage. Intermarriage between *colonos* and *comunarios* and both Llamacacheños and *comunario* enclaves within the hacienda occurred, apart from the historical reasons already given, for the following reasons: a hacienda man sometimes married a *comunaria* who had inherited land because there were only female heirs in her family, or to free himself from the hacienda obligations; on the contrary, sometimes a poor *comunario* married a rich hacienda woman to gain entry into the hacienda while still retaining whatever land he inherited in the *comunidad*. Bonds were also established between Llamacachi and the adjacent section of Chua in part because a few Chua families were settled in Llamacachi when Llamacachi was assimiliated by Chua for nine years, and in part because this section of Chua holds pasture land adjacent to that of Llamacachi where adolescent shepherds from both communities had frequent occasion to meet each other. For the latter reason Cawaya intermarried with this same Chua section as well.

Marriages with sections of other communities mark potential lines of community cleavage. Thus, in 1967, Llamacachi and Cawaya both decided to change county affiliation. Prior to that date they had belonged to the same county as the other Compi sections, but at present they are part of the recently established Chua county. At the same time, however, marriage ties prevent disputes among intermarrying sections from becoming too severe, since, as we have observed in the last chapter and shall have occasion to see again in the next, they demand interaction between families from different sections and each section as a whole.

A quarrel between Llamacachi and Compi over land which some *comunarios* had acquired from the patrón of Compi is an example of mediation through relatives on both sides of an intersectional dispute.

The reason this quarrel occurred is a deep-rooted sense of difference which the *comunarios* believe distinguishes them from the ex-*colonos*. They have always looked down upon the ex-*colonos* who worked like serfs for a patrón, while the Compeños felt that this was an honorable way of life. The sense of difference extends also to the handful of *comunarios* in Tauca, Kalamaya, and Cawaya. Although they intermarry quite freely with their ex-*colono* neighbors and attend their meetings, they still belong to Llamacachi and they even continue to furnish authorities for Llamacachi.

Now and then hostilities break out between *comunarios* and ex-*colonos*. Such was the case in the second half of 1965. A dispute arose over a piece of hacienda land which the patrón has sold to people from Llamacachi and to *comunarios* from Tauca. Even though at the time Compeños showed no interest in purchasing all the land the patrón was allowed to retain, they now objected to this sale.

Trouble began when the persons from Llamacachi, having purchased such parcels of land between the road and the lake, started planting on the cattle tracks used by the Compeños for driving their cattle to the lake shore, in this way impeding free passage to the lake. A few ex-*colonos* who felt particularly aggravated began collecting signatures of all the local persons who desired land possessed by Llamacacheños. The matter was then elevated to the community level. When some of the Llamacachi families refused to sell the land, it was decided to take the land by force.

This action was recommended by the Compi lawyer. (How was he going to start a lawsuit if Llamacachi and Compi remained on good terms?) First the boys from Compi drove all the animals belonging to Llamacachi out of the disputed territory. Then all the families from the five zones brought a few pounds of broad beans and their teams of oxen and started to plow and sow in the parcels belonging to the *comunarios* including those from Tauca, Kalamaya, and Cawaya. Except for some stone throwing between a small group of Compeños and one Llamacachi family, no resistance was offered on the part of Llamacachi. A few days later a commission from the Ministry of Peasant Affairs arrived to establish the basis of Llamacachi's complaints. The same night a fire destroyed a house in Capilaya, and Llamacachi was of course suspected. In addition, people from both Compi proper and Capilaya were arrested in La Paz, and they had to pay high sums for bail. A bicycle belonging to a person from Tauca was found totally dismantled in Llamacachi. This kindled tempers in Compi even more and made them determined to fight it out with Llamacachi. Moreover, the cost of the paper war, which had started in La Paz in the meantime, grew more and more onerous, and Compeños felt that they could not afford to pay Llamacachi for their land even if they would agree to sell it. Finally, Compi cut off all irrigation water.

Assemblies in Compi proper and Capilaya continued, slowly tiring the leaders, and the dispute might well have come to an end if the *intendente*, a county deputy who was himself a Compeño, had not continued to instigate the ex-*colonos*. He had a personal interest in the continuation of the struggle because he accumulated a handsome reward from it as he collected considerable sums of money, part of which he kept for himself, for bribing all sorts of officials. By threatening to withdraw or even to change sides he could always press more money out of the community.

Finally, Llamacachi decided to take drastic action. The police brigade from Achacachi, the provincial capital, was called, and a dozen soldiers herded together the family heads of the entire ex-hacienda. The hearings which followed did not bear any results, however, because the Compeños said that the matter had been brought before the authorities in La Paz and therefore Achacachi had no right to interfere. This was not far from the truth; the quarrel had been taken up by at least *three* offices in La Paz: the Prefecture, the Ministry of Peasant Affairs, and the National Council for Agrarian Reform. Thus the struggle continued both in Achacachi and in La Paz without much progress toward settlement. Usually when hearings were held in Achacachi only one of the two parties involved would appear, and thus the case would have to be postponed again. Bribes continued to flow freely and the quarrel became more and more costly for both parties.

Then at the end of December, 1965, the *intendente* ordered the ex-*colonos* to harvest the unripe barley growing in the disputed fields. Even though it could at best serve as cattle fodder, everyone harvested as much as he could. This in turn led to ill feeling among the families and between the sections in Compi who felt they had received less than their share. When we left Compi in January, 1966, some Compeños wanted the land to be divided among all the ex-*colonos*, which would scarcely have given each person a furrow of land, while others preferred to have the land divided among those who were most interested in the purchase. Even among the ex-*colonos*, consensus could not be established.

About half a year later the squabble did end however. Not only were the parties tired of the onerous litigations but a few Llamacacheños with close relatives in Compi and all the *comunario* enclaves within the ex-hacienda wished to make peace and offered to sell the land they had acquired. Later most of the others followed suit. Thanks to the network of kinship ties which repaired the differences, the ties between *comunidad* and ex-hacienda had never been entirely severed.

Even though hostilities were suspended the resentment continues to produce incidents from time to time. Thus Llamacacheños, who wish to build their own school, had to be forced to help in the construction of new teachers' quarters in Compi by threats of forced labor in a nearby military establishment.

The relationships between the ex-hacienda sections are not always harmonious either, as can be seen from the recent history of Compi leadership. After the agrarian reform a joint syndicate was established with delegates from every ex-hacienda section. At its head was the *secretario general*; among the other 11 positions there was the *secretario de agricultura* who took over the ritual functions of the pre-reform *jilakata*, the secretary of sports who organized the community soccer team and the *secretario de actas* who kept the members' list. The other secretaries had functions in name only. However, this joint syndicate was of short duration since the bond created by sharing the feudal labor obligations was no longer present. In the first years after the reform, the struggle to expropriate the hacienda land from the patrón did for a time unite all Compeños, but even at that time the sections began sharecropping the hacienda land in their territory separately. Soon the Compeños became convinced that the secretary-general was acting too much in the exclusive support of his own section, Tauca. Had he not had a map of the whole ex-hacienda made, which even included Llamacachi, under the title "Ex-*comunidad* Tauca"? But the straw that broke the camel's back was when the peasants of Compi proper presented a sack of specially-selected potatoes from the hacienda land in *their* section to the President of the Republic and the secretary-general offered it in the name of the "Ex-*comunidad Tauca*." Thereupon Compi proper and Capilaya decided to form a separate unit of their own, leaving only Tauca, Kalamaya, and Cawaya under the jurisdiction of the "selfish" secretary-general.

But problems were soon to arise to harass the remaining unity even of these last two ancient hacienda sections. For one thing, Capilaya was expropriated entirely and Compi only in part, and thus Capilaya was freed entirely from the bonds still tieing it to the patrón, while Compi was not. Moreover, a dispute arose over the land which Capilaya claimed it had always owned. In all this, therefore, continuing to act as one unit with Compi became unattractive to them. The result was that the two sections began having separate meetings.

In their turns, too, Kalamaya and Cawaya separated themselves from Tauca more gradually. After the expropriation had been terminated and the titles to the land had been distributed, the secretary-general ceased to attend the meetings in Cawaya. The two secretaries of Cawaya, the secretary of sports and the secretary of finance, led the assemblies until 1967 when Cawaya formed a separate syndicate. Kalamaya also ceased to recognize the secretary-general of Tauca, the same man who had offended Compi and who had not been changed since the office was created. They too felt that he was only attending to matters concerning his own section. Today there is no secretary-general in Kalamaya, only a *jilakata* and a few other secretaries. The *alcalde escolar* there holds considerable sway even in matters not concerning the school. This seems to be a carry-over from the first years after the reform, when the *alcalde escolar* represented the people of Kalamaya in the syndicate.

Today the school and, as we shall see later, the fiestas are the main interests which are shared by all the different sections. However, were it not for marriage ties, these interests would probably not be able to keep each section from going completely separate paths. As things are in Compi today most matters concern the sections alone. They are dealt with in meetings where all married men belonging to the section are allowed to participate.

Decision Making

These assemblies take place on a special meeting ground: the *ala pata*[1] which is near the center of the community. Since the houses in Compi are fairly close together, most of them are within shouting distance of the *ala pata*. The meetings take place either in the morning between eight and ten o'clock or in the

---

[1] *Ala pata* literally means "buying place." Vendors who visit the community sell their wares there. During the feast of "alasitas" people bring small quantities of produce and animals made out of *quinua* meal, and play at marketing there.

evening before the sun sets. The secretary-general and the *jilakata* are the first to arrive at the gathering place. They have to wait patiently, sometimes for hours, until the family heads have assembled. From time to time they call out, in order to be assured that everyone has heard; the main topic to be discussed is also announced; and to attract people it is sometimes even rendered more dramatic by adding a few white lies. Never do *all* the family heads convene. When a sufficient number of persons are present, or when it is thought that no one more will be coming, the assembly starts. Frequently more arrive during the course of the discussion.

Significant differences exist among the sections with respect to the ease with which people assemble. In Capilaya they convene quickly and there is usually a high attendance rate, while in Compi it is so much more difficult to get the people together that, frequently, meetings are postponed or dropped altogether.

The weight carried by individual section members in the decision-making process depends primarily on seniority and the position of an individual in the prestige system of the community. These two criteria usually go together, since it takes time for a man to fulfill the various political charges and fiesta sponsorships on which prestige is based. For instance, Lino Nacho at the age of 38 has been a secretary of justice, secretary-general, president of the neighborhood council and sponsor of a number of feasts. Therefore his opinions carry weight. Equally, magical talents are of considerable importance for political influence, especially when the magician serves the community in rain-bringing and hail-preventing ceremonies (see Chapter 7). However, a person should know how to express himself diplomatically and well. Persons who possess these abilities are listened to even if they have not yet fulfilled sufficient political and ritual obligations to merit the full status of an elder. They are given political positions which demand energetic personalities. Further criteria for political weight are education and connections in the La Paz bureaucracy, qualities which are not associated with seniority in Compi. We will be concerned with the role of such educated persons in the community and county further on in this chapter.

Although many persons with the highest prestige have assumed the position of secretary-general in Compi, this position does not necessarily require a very advanced prestige standing. As a matter of fact, sometimes persons are elected simply because they have been particularly critical of their predecessors. This is done in order to silence them in future years. During the first years after the agrarian reform in the litigations against the patrón, it was essential that at least one important leader in each section be able to speak Spanish, but afterwards older, unilingual Aymara speakers were preferred again.

Decisions are arrived at by consensus; if one or two persons should disagree adamantly in a given case, the solution usually has to be altered, or sometimes the problem is left unsolved. Then the question is postponed for the next meeting or simply dropped.

In Capilaya, consensus is usually achieved quite quickly and although people may disagree, a satisfactory outcome is usually possible; therefore meetings are short. But in Compi proper, a few persons dissent, as it were, out of principle. When such persons are present, agreement is difficult. Interestingly, the main troublemakers in Compi proper belong to two definite categories: opportunists among the migrants in La Paz who desire to enrich themselves at the expense of fellow Compeños and their relatives in Compi whom they succeed in winning for their cause, and persons who do not seem to be entirely normal. Examples of the last type are Ambrosio and Lucho.

Ambrosio had the habit of talking against all the *secretarios*. He never paid his quotas and if a *secretario* would explain some project, he would be sure to find something to say against it. As our assistant Paz recounts with disgust: "The assembly just waits for one dissenting voice and like the herd of sheep which says 'baa' when just one sheep says 'baa,' the assembly listens to Ambrosio and becomes disconcerted by his objections." Ambrosio has occasional epileptic seizures even during assemblies. Similarly, Lucho is believed to be of an unstable mentality. His technique of sowing dissent is somewhat different: he voices objections and then simply leaves *ala pata*. In his case the technique of nominating him as secretary-general was adopted. The method worked. Lucho has not been causing trouble recently.

Perpetual dissent, of course, affects the morale of the whole community, and it is certainly one of the main reasons for the lack of enthusiasm for assemblies. Everyone in Compi is happy when the dissenters cannot attend, for then they can resolve the issues.

Some persons stay away from assemblies habitually. One such person cultivates as much cooperative land as he pleases, not heeding the decisions made in the assemblies. Others do not attend because they are unmarried, and still others keep away from assemblies because they are Protestants.

Absenteeism from meetings is especially serious in Llamacachi where a high proportion of the population are Baptists. There, a few very able persons fail to make any considerable impact on the community because they do not attend assemblies. Perhaps this is due to the fact that their religion impedes their taking part in many of the community's religious concerns like feasts and magical performances. Therefore they prefer to stay in the background in order to diminish tension and avoid being criticized.

Everyone enjoys the right to voice his opinion in assemblies, but if very young men or former *mayorunis* (the lowest category of hacienda serfs) take the floor too frequently, they are criticized by their elders. Women are excluded except on occasions when they substitute for their husbands. In Compi, for instance, a woman on one occasion requested that her husband be nominated as sponsor of the brass band in a coming fiesta. They may also appear as litigants or as witnesses.

The discussion during assemblies passes from one subject to another. If the going becomes too hard, the topic is changed and the dropped topic may be taken up again later. Hotheaded discussions are usually avoided, since the Aymara usually argue or fight only under the influence of alcohol.

In Llamacachi community meetings follow a similar pattern. Leadership has changed but little since the agrarian reform with the exception that all obligations toward the former county seat, including the weekly briefings, have been abolished. The only new addition to the political hierarchy was the *presidente de la junta vecinal*, or president of the neighborhood or town council. This position was originally associated with villages and city neighborhoods alone. However, recently the position was created in dispersed settlements as well, in emulation of the villages. While in Compi the *presidente* acts as principal school authority, in Llamacachi his jurisdiction extends much farther. He attends all the assemblies and gives advice on such diverse problems as irrigation or church building. This *presidente*, who has been in charge ever since the creation of the post, seems to have attained authority thanks to his schooling in La Paz. Indeed, in his case, the position of *presidente de la junta vecinal* is important simply because of his influence in the community. His activities as a judge in the community later helped him attain the post of *intendente*, or head of the cantón for the year 1964. In this way the *jilakata* has lost more and more of his influence, especially in the last few years. Increasingly, disputes which formerly would have been settled by him were brought either to the *presidente de la junta vecinal*, to the *intendente* in Jank'o Amaya, or directly to the authorities in La Paz.

The creation of an authority higher than the *jilakata* has not increased cohesion in Llamacachi. While the schism between the Catholics and the Protestants continued and the rivalry between the two principal families was still remembered, there was no real necessity to settle disputes at the local level. The traditional authorities could easily be bypassed and the dispute settled on the cantón level or in La Paz. Previous to the military coup, political rallies organized by the M.N.R. party had at least forced the *comunarios* to hold meetings now and then. However, the military coup ended all such rallies in the community. Thus there had not been a single assembly between November 1964 and October 1965. A meeting was finally called on October 21, 1965, in order to decide about a joint project with the neighboring ex-hacienda Chua to construct a school latrine.

In order to give an idea of how difficult it is for Llamacacheños to reach any decision at all, we shall give here an almost literally translated recording of this one assembly:

October 21st, 1965: We came upon the meeting by chance at five o'clock in the afternoon with Sofia, one of our interpreters.

Many of the men were assembled already and Mariano, an old man, asked the assembly bitterly why the *presidente de la junta vecinal* had been reviling him. It seems that the *presidente* had constructed an irrigation ditch across the land of a widow. When she came to protest he had told her that the ditch was more advantageous to Torribio and Mariano's son. The assembly listened with sympathy to the complaints of the old man: "What a bad character the *presidente* has! And now he has not even come to the assembly. He must assuredly be at fault if he does not appear." "I have seen him talk with Tiburcio," added Mariano. "We thought that Tiburcio was his enemy and now he acts like a traitor towards us." "Well," said the others, "let's wait until 'el Loco Mister' (the *presidente's* nickname) comes and clarifies what had happened."

Máximo, the school *alcalde*, then spoke up: "The *señorita* (director of the Baptist schools in the area) asks that tomorrow four men come to help build latrines for the school in Chua (a program started by a Peace Corps volunteer)." "We have heard about this already," answered the assembly, "but the branch of the Baptist school in Compi is giving exams tomorrow and we want to attend those." "We have commitments to the schools in both Chua and Compi," protested Máximo. "Only four persons are needed. The rest can go to Compi."

No decision could be reached, and some beckoned to us to sit in the center and asked how they could irrigate the community. "You have been here for a long time and know the situation: both Compi and Chua do not want to permit us to use water from their springs and streams. Could one pump water up to a reservoir from the lake? How much would a pump cost and how long would the pipe have to be?" "Everyone would be in agreement to pay quotas for buying a pump," added Crisóstomo, a relative of a Llamacachi family who had come from La Paz to help settle a family dispute. We told them that Wayne, the Peace Corps volunteer, would be very willing to inquire about a pump in La Paz, but that we would suggest purchasing a new pump if there was no mechanic in the community.

At this point the *presidente* finally arrived and rather pompously greeted the assembly, remarking how pleasantly surprised he was that the *junta vecinal* had gathered once again. "This is rather remarkable, for when an assembly was called to discuss the epidemiological survey, nobody came, and when el Señor Wayne tried to gather the people, he too found it impossible. We here in Llamacachi are not united: everybody is against everybody else." He then was asked to explain what had occurred with the irrigation canal. This he proceeded to do in a confident voice of authority. "Yes, I have made this canal and it was for this same widow's sake; for she gains most advantage. Water was accumulating on her lands, endangering her crops." "Yes," interrupted Mariano, "but I have heard that you have said bad things against me." The *presidente* continued to explain that he himself had wanted to make an assembly in accordance with the desire of the widow and that it had been impossible to call the people together. The irate Mariano continued interrupting but he was silenced by the *presidente* who shouted at him that he had not yet finished talking. The assembly likewise admonished him to speak politely and to be respectful of the assembled men. "Once, when Mariano's wife was drunk," continued the *presidente*, "she insulted me to my face, telling me that I have a large nose." "Yes," laughed the others, "but she was drunk and you should not take this seriously."

The dispute continued for a while; then the discussion switched to another topic, an argument over a parcel of land. A woman who had been married twice and who had children from both marriages was living with her illegitimate son whom she had conceived by her former husband's brother after her husband's death. They were constructing a new house for themselves on a parcel of land which one of the daughters also desired. The two disputing parties had hurled insults at each other as best they could and then both had gone to La Paz—the illegitimate son to his uncle Crisóstomo and the daughter's husband to a lawyer, who wrote a long history of the case and had an order signed by the *fiscal* to stop construction of the house. The *intendente* of Jank'o Amaya had failed to obtain the signed consent of the illegitimate son to refrain from building, and the community was making a last attempt to settle the matter, feeling that it was ridiculous for the parties to bring such a minor matter to court in La Paz, spending more on lawyers than the disputed parcel of land was worth. Crisóstomo had decided to come to Llamacachi to try to arbitrate the matter; for was he not a relative of both parties?

After hearing the testimonies of the different persons involved, the *presidente* spoke up: "Let the assembly discuss the case and suggest solutions and let me give my opinion at the end; for if I speak now, even if my verdict is just, I shall be criticized by you, for I know that you dislike me." The *jilakatas* did not want to decide the issue either, but encouraged the people to speak. The older men were then asked to give their opinions. Some suggested that the land be divided immediately among the illegitimate son and the two legitimate daughters of the second husband whose land it had been originally. Others asked that the illegitimate son and his mother be allowed to continue with the construction of the house and that the mother should decide later whether or not to pass the house on to her son, depending on how well he took care of her.

Then an aunt of one of the daughters spoke up: "Let me say a few words, let me tell you the truth about this woman. She left her husband on his deathbed and did not even bother to attend his funeral. She did this on purpose in order to disinherit her daughters. Finally she had this illegitimate child. The daughters should inherit all the land and not the son." An angry murmur rose from the assembly: "You should not pronounce such words about things past. She had a right to live at her father's home after the death of her husband. Also, it is more than common that a widow finds herself with child. Moreover, is it the fault of the young man? He is of age now and should be allowed to build a house for himself and his mother."

A young man from the community who had become a teacher admonished the two parties to be sensible: "If the question is not settled here and you go to court, then you shall have to pay large sums of money to the lawyers and to the judges. The dispute over the land which I am having with the people of Compi is costing me more than a million bolivianos. Where are you going to get this money? The parcel is worth only about 800,000 Bs."[2]

Finally it was decided to call an assembly in the morning to divide the land. The daughter's husband left saying that he did not have time in the morning, and as we heard later only four persons gathered the next day, so the problem could not be solved.

The assembly was about to break up when the *alcalde escolar* called out desperately: "Wait, I called this assembly to discuss the question of the school latrines." "That is your own fault, why didn't you bring this up in the beginning?" answered the rest.

The the *presidente* spoke up: "It would be a shame if this question were not solved. What would our neighbors in Chua say if we are thus disunited?"[3] The *alcalde* added: "The *señorita* from Huatajata asked me for four men. I have to comply with her orders. The school in Chua was founded thanks only to the participation of Llamacachi, but if we fail in our obligation toward it, the name of Llamacachi shall be erased from the school facade. Do not laugh at me, I have not called the assembly in order that you could discuss all sorts of other things." "Go tell the *señorita* that we will *all* come on *Saturday*." "That is impossible, the *señorita* said that it had to be on Friday, and that four persons are enough." "Well, tell the *señorita* to fire you from your office then."

The *presidente* then admonished the people to be sensible and they answered: "Yes, we have been *alcaldes escolares* ourselves and we know what is right." However, only two persons finally volunteered to go while most of the men left for their homes, as it was already dark.

Some continued to talk about irrigation problems. Compi had not only taken away the land which they had purchased from the former patrón (see pp. 52–53) but had also cut off their water supply. After deciding to postpone action until tempers in Compi had cooled, everyone went home.

The topics discussed in the Llamacachi meeting are typical of Compi concerns. The main topics in all assemblies, both the sectional ones and those of the whole ex-hacienda, concern the school and land. In the first few years after the

---

[2] The boliviano was replaced by the peso boliviano in 1956, worth 1000 bolivianos. Most Bolivians have not switched to the new currency entirely in their thinking.

[3] The possibility of being looked down upon by the people of the neighboring ex-hacienda Chua because of the disunity in the community was expressed a number of times during the assembly.

reform, land was first in importance and was discussed in an endless series of assemblies. As a matter of fact, land was so crucial that it was more expedient to have the secretary-general reside in La Paz, to deal with the authorities there, than to have him present in the community where a substitute acted in his stead in assemblies. During the period of our study the school was the most important topic. This topic concerns the community as a whole. However, the community does not hold general meetings, except in the circumstances of emergency as once, during the quarrel between Llamacachi and Compi, when the five ex-hacienda sections gathered as a threatening gesture against the *comunarios*. Rather, the presidents of the neighborhood councils from each section, other school authorities, a handful of persons interested in the problem to be discussed, and sometimes a secretary-general or two meet in front of the school for discussion. Later the presidents and the secretaries-general call special meetings in each section or mention their case in assemblies convened for other reasons. Finally the presidents announce the results in general school authority meetings once more. If consensus can not be attained, yet another series of section meetings has to be held.

In fact this system of referrals has flaws. Often no representatives of one or more sections were present. However, those who were present usually were already acquainted with the position of those who were absent. Thus commissions could be nominated to visit the dissenting sections in order to gain their acquiescence. Nevertheless, each school authority has some power to decide issues without an additional assembly in its zone each time.

The Role of Migrants in the Community

The Llamacachi meeting also provides a good example of the role of migrants in the community. Both the *presidente* and Crisóstomo have lived in La Paz. The *presidente* has returned to Llamacachi permanently while Crisostomo visits the community occasionally.

The *presidente*, whom we shall call Damian, and his wife have probably exercised the deepest influence on Llamacachi. Damian has received eighth grade education in La Paz. His wife came from La Paz originally where she was adopted and brought up by a missionary couple who took her to Canada for three years; therefore, she speaks good English. She attended secondary school, too. Both interrupted their studies when they got married and went to Llamacachi. Damian's wife is frequently consulted for illness, for she is able to give injections and to cure minor ailments. Her advice and cooperation prove invaluable for adjustments of dance costumes. Similarly, she gives counsel on family quarrels and is generally respected for her knowledge of the *mestizo* world. In a sense she keeps aloof from the mainstream of Llamacachi life. She yearns to work in the United States and is now looking for a job there. She and her husband established the first school in Llamacachi some 30 years ago and constructed one of the first houses with a corrugated iron roof and large windows. They even owned a piano. Damian himself was Llamacachi's first Baptist preacher. However, he became involved in litigations with the other important Llamacachi family, and a quarrel ensued which split the community for many years. It is not certain that there had been more community spirit in Llamacachi before the feud, but if this were the case, the community has never recovered. Damian's knowledge of judiciary matters was useful to Llamacachi when its neighbors prevented the irrigation water from flowing into the community. He was one of the only persons to warn the community against misman-agement of funds by the leaders of the purchasing cooperative. His experience and his knowledge of politics contributed to his election as *intendente* of Jank'o Amaya for 1964. Then when Chua created its own county in December, 1966, he became its first *corregidor*. Even when not in office he is frequently sought for advice in judiciary matters. In spite of his prominent position in the community, he, like his wife, does not feel completely part of it. During assemblies his outspoken-ness is resented by fellow Llamacacheños, for the Aymara pattern is not to tread on too many toes, at least when one is sober. He, too, would like to follow his wife to the United States if she succeeds in finding a position there. His sons and daugh-ters are studying in La Paz or are learning professions there; they all wear *mestizo* clothes and have little contact with Llamacacheños. Even their pattern of child care is different. Damian, his family, and his son-in-law's family who have lived in the community since the fall of the M.N.R. in 1966, form a different social stratum marked by a different drinking pattern and a different outlook toward life. One feels that they are stranded in the country and would prefer to return to city life. They are viewed with ambivalence by their countrymen—on the one hand re-spected and needed but on the other hand regarded with suspicion.

In Compi, migrants have played an important role in community politics as well. Pascual, for example, is one of the most influential migrants in Compi. He left for La Paz in 1941 when his father could no longer endure the hardships of hacienda life. There he continued his education to the sixth grade which he had begun in Huatajata. In 1945, he returned to Compi with the rest of the family. The life of his family was affected but little by the four years of living in La Paz. Pascual's father worked harder than ever before to the admiration of his country-men who told him that he must have learned how to work like that in La Paz. The only change seems to have been in tastes for food and clothing. The family ate more rice, noodles and other non-Compi staples which the average Compeño only used to consume during feast days. Pascual's sisters had learned some new ways of preparing food when they worked as servants in La Paz. Also, more and more the family came to rely on purchased cloth for making clothing rather than weaving it themselves. Pascual's education and good manners were invaluable to the patrón who asked him to take stock of the harvest and act as a servant during his large parties in Compi and in Sorata.

However, it was just after the agrarian reform that Pascual's superior edu-cation and acculturation became more important. He was the one to initiate the process of expropriation of Compi, and for years he lived in La Paz holding various Compi leadership positions, fighting a paper war against the former patrón. Later he and his relative Pedro, whose contributions to the community shall be analyzed later, and 12 other Compeños and Llamacacheños entered an agreement with the son of the patrón to cultivate part of the hacienda as a cooperative. Finally, he enlisted the aid of a Catholic institution for whom he was working, to construct a school in Compi.

However, Pascual's sojourn in La Paz made him feel less at ease in the country, so he worked first in La Paz and later in Cochabamba. Even after his return to the community in 1954 when his mother died, he continues to feel nostalgic about other places, especially for Cochabamba. He planted cherry trees like those he had seen in Cochabamba, wears a Cochabamba hat, and his new house looks remarkably like the houses around Cochabamba. Thus, even though he is very much respected by Compeños and sits with elders during fiestas, he feels somewhat out of place in Compi. This fact certainly contributed to his acceptance of the position of interpreter and investigator. After a few months he was able to present his own theories about aspects of Compi life, which is possible only for persons who are somewhat disassociated from the center of a community's activities.

Later he worked in La Paz where he initiated contacts among the lower echelons in the government bureaucracy which may prove helpful to the development of the community. For instance, when the authors were studying market syndicates in La Paz, he became friendly with the secretary-general of the market syndicate confederation. After we left, this person was asked to become a legal advisor for Compeños.

The Compi and Llamacachi migrant community and the persons in La Paz with whom they have contacts are in a very concrete sense extensions of the community just as individual Compeños in La Paz are active members of extended families in Compi.

County Politics

County politics depend on migrants to an even greater extent. The same persons who act as intermediaries between the community and authorities in La Paz are also potential candidates for top level political positions on the county level. At least for the *intendente*, or judge, it is essential to possess a knowledge of Spanish and to be able to read and write, or be aided by someone who has these faculties. Since the *intendente* is expected to make improvements in the county capital, such as initiating the construction of a church or establishing a telegraph connection, contacts with sources of funds in La Paz are desirable as well. It is therefore not surprising that all but one of the annually appointed *intendentes* (this exception was a Pazeño) had lived in La Paz at one time. Damian's case, given above, is typical. He was able to fulfill his term in office as *intendente* of Jank'o Amaya without any help, thanks to his schooling in La Paz. He also keeps up with the developments in national politics and has a working knowledge of the legal code which he studies in his spare time. Another *intendente*, whom I shall call Fabian, had to depend on the aid of Mr. A., a predecessor who considers himself a scribe, with whom Fabian had to share his revenues in fees and fines.

The *intendente* is a busy man. Every Thursday he has to go to Jank'o Amaya to preside over hearings on disputes ranging from marriage difficulties to quarrels over land. Even when he is at home on his *sayaña*, people come to his

house with complaints; at least in theory, he should be available in his office during the entire week. His actual powers are, of course, limited. For example, in cases
of theft or other major offenses, he may not imprison a suspect for more than 24
hours, after which he must take him to La Paz. Moreover, if the parties involved
in a quarrel are not satisfied with the *intendente's* verdict, they can always appeal
to the authorities in La Paz. Disputes over land, for instance, are usually settled
by the National Council for Agrarian Reform in La Paz or by the Ministry of
Peasant Affairs.

In order to give an idea of an *intendente's* task let us describe, from our
notes, the happenings at the police office on one Thursday morning during Fabian's
term in office.

When we came into the police office at ten o'clock in the morning on
Thursday, October 14, 1965, both the *intendente* and Mr. A. were very occupied with hearings; two or three cases had already been settled earlier and a
number of persons were waiting in the office for their turn. Four cases were being
tried simultaneously: the school authorities from the Baptist school in Compi
wanted to have a document signed for the continuation of the school in the next
school year; a *mestizo* demanded payment of damages for the destruction of his
store by drunkards; a Compeño was upset because a man from Chua whom he did
not like particularly had run off with his daughter (the normal practice in Compi
to secure oneself a wife) and wanted to marry her. Finally a couple, who had been
separated for a number of years, was entering an agreement that their son live
with the father. These four cases, interspersed by simpler ones which were handled
in a few minutes, occupied the entire morning.

The case about the school was soon postponed until later, but the demand
for payment of damages created more problems. Evidently it had all started a month
earlier when four persons entered into the store of the *mestizo*, wrecking the place.
Only one of the culprits, Domingo, presented himself in the *intendencia* and he
wanted to pay only for one fourth of the damage. The *mestizo* came into the
police office demanding that the *intendente* compel obedience. This hurt the feelings
of the *intendente* who shouted back at the *mestizo* that he should show some respect when he entered his office. Then Domingo's guarantor graciously offered
to cancel the sum right there and then, but the discussion continued until the
mestizo left the office. Mr. A. suggested quietly that the three other culprits be
called, and, when this proved impossible, the guarantor, who was a friend of the
intendente, changed his mind about being guarantor—although he had agreed in
writing earlier—and Mr. A. remarked pleasantly: "Oh well, now the store owner
can try to have the damage paid himself."

In the meantime the *intendente* was also grappling with the case of
Agustin, the Compeño. It seems that the father of the boy who had run off with
his daughter had made the customary visit to his house in order to explain what
had happened and in order to talk about the marriage. He had come, as the custom
prescribes, with a *chino* or bottle of alcohol tied up with a cloth with coca. However,
he had made the mistake of visiting Agustin in a rather tipsy state and when it became evident that Agustin was none too pleased with the prospect of the marriage,
a brawl ensued.

Jank'o Amaya, the county seat, during the weekly fair. The building at the extreme right is the church. At the extreme left lie the school and the soccer field.

Agustin knew of course that he could not prevent the marriage without bringing shame to his daughter, but he demanded that a person be found who would act as a guarantor in case the marriage did not succeed, since, because of the inauspicious beginning, the marriage could easily end in a quarrel between the families of the future spouses. The *intendente* advised the men who presented themselves as guarantors to keep their hands off the matter because the bridegroom's family was notorious for quarreling. Thus the discussion between the two parties became more and more involved.

The boy's father then declared unctuously: "Agustin's daughter came to our home of her own free will and I cannot throw her out. The next day I went to speak to Agustin. I admit that I was drunk but I cannot remember if I have insulted Agustin in his home or not." But Agustin and especially his wife were still not satisfied, for not only had the boy's father insulted Agustin, but he had looked for a marriage *padrino* in Chua when the prerogative of naming the godfather should belong to the bride's family. The *padrino* named by the boy's father stood up and demanded that he be paid for his loss of honor if the padrinoship were to be canceled.

The discussion continued confusedly. Agustin had sent a note to his brother in La Paz, who had gone to the police there, but the police referred the case to the *intendente* in Jank'o Amaya. The father of the boy exclaimed bitterly that his son would go to prison if necessary. Finally, they all left the office and later we found them walking back home together probably arranging the matter among themselves.

At the same time the *intendente* and Mr. A. were also studying the fourth case. The man and his wife, from whom he had separated several months earlier, were haggling over the sum the husband would pay for his son. Also, a list of objects had to be checked which were supposed to have belonged to the wife. The wife had a document from the child welfare association in La Paz according to which the husband owed her an alimony of 1,800,000 bolivianos (150 dollars). The discussion continued during the whole morning and well into the afternoon until the sum was painfully extracted from the husband.

During a lull Mr. A. brought up a case of his own against a Tauqueño called Juan. The man had come into his shop completely drunk and had insulted him when he was told that no beer was available. "I would have beaten Juan if I weren't a gentleman," said A. Juan, after protesting that he had done no such thing, finally did sign a promise of good conduct, and thus the honor of Mr. A. was assuaged. A number of other cases were treated thereafter, concerning land, a hat that had been kicked away by someone, and so on. The office was closed at three in the afternoon.

In the three sessions we attended, the most frequent issues were quarrels over land that occur, for instance, when an illegitimate or an adopted child demands a share of the family inheritance or when a person plows farther than the edge of his field, and drunken brawls which have resulted in personal injury, damage to property, or sometimes insults. Other issues included quarrels between spouses and subsequent separation, debts and accident claims.

Post-reform *cantón* politics do not depend on officials alone, but on complete processes of fission and fusion.

Before the reform Compi and Llamacachi belonged to the *cantón* of Santiago de Huata which included a great number of communities on the peninsula of the same name and some adjacent territory. *Cantones* tended to be large but, as we have mentioned before, the power of the *corregidores* at the head of the *cantones* was limited largely to free communities. If the *corregidores* exercised authority at all in the hacienda it was mostly in favor of the patrones.

After the reform a curious process of splitting took place. Any community which had been able to establish a weekly market in its territory or had built a small village consisting of a group of houses around a plaza, considered itself eligible as capital of a *cantón*. Thus the larger villages, whose prerogative it had previously been, found their jurisdiction shrinking more and more, while new villages were mushrooming all over around new market places whose development we have analyzed already. Jank'o Amaya, the ex-hacienda bordering Compi to the north was in a good position to become a *cantón* capital. It was large, was situated far from the nearest market, and was in need of an outlet for its large potato crop. Step by step it succeeded in gaining economic and political primacy over its neighbors. However, all the other larger communities aspired to become *cantón* capitals as well. They feel that the *cantón* capitals have all the advantages and progress. Thus Chua, after many years of trying, has finally been able to attain the status of accessory *cantón*. Compi has thus far been unsuccessful. Establishing a rival market with Jank'o Amaya is out of the question since Compeños sell their cash crop, onions, directly in La Paz so they hope to persuade La Paz authorities to recognize a separate judge in the county seat.

Since the boundaries of the *cantones* are not well defined, problems concerning the spheres of influence of different peasant leaders are apt to arise between the *intendentes* and the authorities at the provincial level. A good illustration of the latter was a theft committed on the border of the *cantón* of Jank'o Amaya and the *cantón* Huatajata. In December, 1964, a boy from Cawaya was found butchering a stolen llama in the house of an accomplice. Somehow the police in Tiquina, another nearby *cantón*, got wind of it and arrived on the scene to raid the house of the accomplice. In Llamacachi, the *intendente* and his supporters, outraged by the interference in their affairs by the police from another *cantón*, took custody of all the plundered articles in the *intendente's* house. The *intendente* had the thief put into prison and attempted thus to learn more about the circumstances of the theft. This in turn enraged the *intendente* of Huatajata who claimed that the place of the theft was under *his* jurisdiction and therefore the investigation of the case was *his* business. Politics entered the affair when the sub-prefect in Achacachi was notified of the crime. The *intendente* of Jank'o Amaya was accused of being a filthy adherent of the party supporting the last regime who plundered homes of innocent persons. Only after ten days was the accused boy finally sent to La Paz.

Apart from the rivalries with other *cantones*, an *intendente's* power is curtailed by his superiors, the sub-prefect of Achacachi, the province capital and the prefect of the *departmento*, or state of La Paz. This limitation is not only due to legal constraints but also to the fact that disputing parties simply take their case to a number of different authorities in La Paz. For, just as the community has a choice of ministries to file a case (as we have seen in the dispute between Compi and Llamacachi), the individual does too. His La Paz relatives will always help him to accomplish this.

*
* *

Section, community and county politics in the Compi area are of an extremely fluid nature. Community politics consist primarily of the sum of decisions resolved in meetings each section holds separately. Thus, sections act as autonomous entities in most matters. Only for certain purposes, such as education or litigation over land between sections, are there efforts in coordinating decision making. Returned migrants are perhaps the only persons capable of such coordination. Their standpoint is sufficiently different from that of the traditional community leaders to preclude competition (for specific tasks requiring knowledge of the national political hierarchy which only they can provide). Returned migrants are given considerable leeway. However, section interests may diverge in spite of the migrants' mediation. In this case, the same phenomenon may occur as in dissent within a section, where each household decides whether or not it will support a common project. For example, just as in a given section, roads may be narrower in spots for years because some individuals refuse to cede any of their land for road construction or fail to carry out their assigned task, a project on the community level may either be abandoned or the sections in favor may proceed to carry out their part in the hope that the dissident sections will eventually follow suit. Outside authorities can only rarely be enlisted to exercise pressure on the dissidents. As a result, Compi community projects such as the school consist of a mosaic of buildings in various stages of construction.

On the county level politics are even more fluid as communities vie with each other to extend their influence by economic as well as political means. While on the section and community levels kinship ties between sections and between sections and migrants to La Paz both influence the outcome of issues, on the county level the position a community is able to secure within the marketing network and the national political hierarchy determines success as a county seat.

Section, community, and county cannot be seen as completely independent levels, however. The community in which the county capital is located has a definite advantage over the other member communities. For instance, houses constructed in the capital may be owned and high political positions may be held by members of the community in which the county seat is located more frequently than by outsiders. Member communities therefore attempt to establish rival county seats on their own territory, thus creating counties with a progressively smaller radius of influence, making differences between county and community less and less significant. Similarly, section interests may prevail over community interests with each section attempting to establish the county capital on its own territory and thus further reducing political jurisdiction.

6

The Fiesta System

C OMPI LIFE CANNOT BE UNDERSTOOD without reference to feast giving. Feast[1] celebration is, apart from education, the only activity in which all the members of the community, including migrants, may be involved at any one time. Because of their inclusive character, feasts provide a common language for all Compeños in which common interests, sectional differences, rivalries and competition can be expressed. In them the division by sections as well as by differences of age, status, political and religious affiliation are reflected, and both continuity and change in social relationships can be communicated, and formal recognition even to newly perceived network regularities be given.

The most important feasts in Compi, the fiestas proper, are those associated with Catholic holidays; the ones which Compeños observe are those connected with the patron saints of the community whose images at the time of the study stood in an unoccupied room of the school awaiting the completion of a large church which was to replace a smaller broken down structure. One image, the Virgin of Charity, was rescued from the hacienda chapel a few years after the agrarian reform before the chapel was demolished along with the rest of the hacienda buildings. In front of the church lies a large plaza where Compeños congregate at the height of the fiestas. Compeños also celebrate a series of life crisis rites beginning at birth and ending with masses for the deceased. Most larger Compi feasts take place during the dry season from May until the beginning of November, which marks a slack in agricultural activities. Even weddings are usually scheduled during this period. The fiesta of the Holy Cross (May 3d), the founding of the school (May 25th), Saint Peter (June 29th), Natividad (September 8th), La Merced (September 24th), and All Saints' (November 1st) all fall within this season. During the wet season, Compeños celebrate New Year's Day, *Alasita*, a fertility rite during which small quantities of produce and animals made out of

---

[1] We shall use the term "fiesta" to designate annually reoccurring adult celebrations and the term "feast" as a more inclusive term designating "fiestas," rites of passage and adolescent rites.

Tauqueño playing the pan-pipes in the ancient mimula *dance which his community section revived for the regional folklore festival.*

quinua meal are sold, Carnival, and Easter. Furthermore, they participate in two fiestas (New Year's Day and Candlemas, February 2d) in neighboring Jank'o Amaya, the county capital.

In all religious fiestas a small number of adult Compeños act as sponsors. This system of sponsorship, or *cargos*, is of Spanish origin and is very widespread in Latin America. It has been adapted to the social organization of the areas in which it was introduced. Sometimes, as in many predominantly *mestizo* communities from Peru to Mexico, sponsors are merely required to canvass the community or city ward for contributions while they themselves have but small expenditures and in some instances may even make a profit. Sometimes religious organizations (*cofradias* and *hermandades*), which may or may not own land, assume the sponsorship function. Finally, individuals may sponsor the fiestas with considerable financial sacrifice. This pattern is perhaps most characteristic of Indian communities in the Andes as well as in Mesoamerica. Usually the *cargos* are hierarchically ranked according to the importance of the feast and the cost involved. Often an individual assumes progressively more onerous and prestigious *cargos*. In many instances, especially in Indian communities, fiesta *cargos* are systematically interlinked with political offices into a politico-religious ladder. Such mixed systems seem to have existed even in pre-Hispanic times. Each political office requires the fulfillment of certain fiesta *cargos* and vice versa. Toward the end of the climb an individual becomes a respected elder in the community, a man whose opinion carries weight in political councils and whose advice is sought by all.

In Compi, during a lifetime an individual is called upon to be responsible for the organization and financing of a number of fiestas of the annual cycle, that is, he must assume a number of specific sponsorships. Invariably he begins with the least taxing ones and ends with the more onerous ones. His status in the community depends to a considerable extent on the number of sponsorships he has assumed in the past, and how many he must still assume to become a *pasado*, a person who has fulfilled all the obligations of the fiesta system. Unlike other Andean and Mesoamerican communities, fiesta *cargos* are not systematically linked with political office. In Compi an individual may enter into the *cargo* or sponsorship system even before he is married with the *cargo* of *cabecilla*, or head of a dance group of Carnival. Sponsorship of this fiesta is open to persons of all ages. However, they may do so only with the consent of their elders.

A *cabecilla's* outlay for Carnival is not much higher than that of the other dancers in his group. The cost of the brass band is shared by all in proportion to their dancing position in the customary two row formations. The first two pay the highest rate, the second two pay somewhat less and so forth, while the last two are usually exempted altogether from sharing the cost since their position has very little prestige attached. The *cabecilla* merely serves alcohol before the other dances and in larger quantities. He also provides more food.

The next rung in the hierarchy is the *cargo* of *cabeza* of the Holy Cross (May 3d). Unlike a *cabecilla*, a *cabeza* assumes the cost of hiring the brass band. Perhaps it is for this reason that most *cabezas* of the Holy Cross merely sponsor an ensemble of flute players from the community itself who never charge for their services and only demand food and cheap cane alcohol rather than the customary beer given brass bands. Whether he sponsors a brass band or not, a *cabeza* must furnish alcohol, coca, and cigarettes for the dancers during the entire fiesta. Moreover, he must feed the dancers and the persons who help him financially. It is inconceivable that a bachelor become a *cabeza* of the Holy Cross. The sponsorship is reserved for married men who generally assume it a few years after marriage, for the wife plays an active part in serving alcohol and food to the wives of the *acompañantes*, or followers.

A year after assuming the *cargo* of *cabeza* of the Holy Cross, a man automatically becomes *preste* of the same fiesta. A *preste* differs from a *cabeza* by the fact that he is not involved in organizing a dance group, but he serves alcohol and food to his followers and during one feast day he is responsible for serving food to the dancers as well. The fiesta of the Holy Cross is but a minor one in Compi and neither the *preste* nor the *cabeza* incur large expenses. Therefore, candidates for the sponsorship frequently prefer to assume both *cargos* simultaneously if the elders of their section permit it, since this is less expensive than consecutive sponsoring. Today young Compi couples usually possess necessary cash for the double sponsorship as a result of the increase in onion production, and thus this option is chosen frequently.

The next step in the religious hierarchy is the *cargo* of *altarero* of Saint Peter (June 29th), the major feast in Compi. The *altarero* constructs a rectangular tent out of poles and woolen blankets on the central plaza. There he serves alcohol and coca during the first day of the fiesta and throughout the following night. He must also feed his retinue as well as the persons who helped him construct the tent. At least in theory this *cargo* is obligatory before proceeding to the two most important sponsorships: *cabeza* and *preste* of Saint Peter. While the expenses of the lower *cargos* are graded according to their importance, this is no longer the case for the higher ones. The *cabeza* sponsorship for Saint Peter is in effect the most costly *cargo* a person can assume, more costly than the subsequent one of *preste* of Saint Peter and far more so than the *cargos* of Natividad. This is due to the fact that the *cabeza* must pay for the services of a brass band and provide beer for it during the entire fiesta. Previous to the introduction of brass bands, some thirty years ago, the *cabeza* had less expenses than the *preste* since, as we have mentioned already, the players of traditional instruments are less demanding. The functions of the *cabeza* of Saint Peter are parallel to those of the *cabeza* of the Holy Cross but on a much larger scale. He has many more dancers and followers to attend.

After *cabeza* of Saint Peter comes *preste* of the same fiesta and finally *cabeza* and *preste* of Natividad.[2] Formerly Natividad was more important than Saint Peter. Today their importance is reversed but the ideal order in which the *cargos* should be assumed has remained unchanged. A final fiesta, Mercedez, whose sponsorships were assumed between those of the Holy Cross and those of Saint Peter has become marginal. Only one section still celebrated this fiesta in 1965.

The fiesta sponsors do not carry the entire burden of the feast themselves. They depend on a system of prestations and counterprestations which links most of the adult members of the community into an intricate network of reciprocal obligations. These prestations are provided in the form of money, beer, bread, fruit, a butchered lamb, and other foodstuffs both to the sponsors of major feasts and life crisis celebrations as well as to persons whose *rites de passage* are being celebrated. The financial aspect of these prestations is not negligible. However, their social aspect is of an equal or greater importance than their financial one. By giving gifts of money and food at a large number of fiestas a man assures himself a large following, for when he sponsors a fiesta in turn the persons to whom he has presented the gifts will return them and participate actively in the celebrations. Even the recruitment of dancers is based on the same principle. A *cabeza* who has previously danced in the dance groups organized by his predecessors can call upon them to dance in his group in turn. In all *rites de passage* participants bring along a pot of soup, a bottle of alcohol, and some coca. This too is considered as *aini*, that is, as a prestation, and must be reciprocated.

Previously a sponsor had to remember all the persons who had made prestations during the fiesta he sponsored. Today he appoints a young man who can read and write to jot down their names and the amounts donated in a notebook. Initial gifts are called *apjjatas*, or *huayños* when they take the form of wreaths of bread and fruit.[3] Gifts given to reciprocate *apjjatas* and *huayños* are called *aini*. The latter term designates the donor as well as gifts and labor exchange in gen-

---

[2] The order in which these four *cargos* are assumed is unimportant in actual fact.
[3] Such wreaths are given as a recompense for service in leadership positions as well.

eral. *Aini gifts should be somewhat larger than the initial gifts*, but the additional amount given does not depend on the time lapse between initial and counter gift. In general, these counter gifts are not directly solicited although this practice does occur occasionally. A recipient may skip a fiesta before returning the prestation without incurring criticism. For instance, he may wait until the donor sponsors a fiesta of equal importance to the one at which the gift was received. In contrast, *cabezas* and *cabecillas* for whom a prospective sponsor has danced may be asked to fulfill their return obligations at the donor's wish. In no instance should a donor force a sponsor to return prestations outside of ritual occasions, although in exceptional cases older community members may give large sums as *apjjatas* to show off their wealth; they seek reimbursement a few days later. Fiesta gift giving thus constitutes a closed system which aids in perpetuating the fiestas: a prospective sponsor must participate in numerous fiestas in order to give a successful one himself and a former sponsor must attend many fiestas subsequently because he must return the *apjjatas* he has received.

A good example of a "career" in feast giving is that of Alberto, a 48-year-old Compeño. Alberto sponsored a fiesta for the first time a year after he became married. During a lunch break while weeding hacienda fields a few months before the fiesta, the hacienda administrator, the *sot'a*, and the *jilakata* from Compi proper discussed likely candidates for the *cabeza* sponsorship of the Holy Cross. "You need not worry," they told Alberto, "all that is required is an *ullucu* soup and some boiled *oca*." Then they sent him home to think the matter over.

Both his father and his brother-in-law encouraged Alberto to assume the sponsorship in spite of the fact that he had incurred many *aini* debts for his marriage. They reasoned that his turn would come within the next few years anyway. Furthermore, they suggested that he assume the *preste* sponsorship simultaneously. In subsequent years, Alberto sponsored two more fiestas in rapid succession: *altarero* of Saint Peter the year after and *altarero* of Natividad the following year. Then, during a syndicate meeting a few years after the agrarian reform, the elders appointed him *cabeza* of Saint Peter. He immediately volunteered for the crowning sponsorship of *preste* of Saint Peter but since there are only three *prestes* for the entire community for this fiesta, the elders obliged him to wait for a number of years. When his turn finally came, Alberto received 11 return gifts from persons to whom he had made gifts on previous occasions and 30 from new donors, of these, 29 were from close, distant, and ritual kin. Although 30 percent of Alberto's *ainis* came from his own section and most live within Compi-Llamacachi, a niece came from Caranavi, a Yungas area where her husband who is not a Compeño himself owns land. Another person, who was visiting with a Compeño offered a gift as well. Three donors came from neighboring communities, a stranger came from Tiquina, a community situated some 15 miles away probably simply to enjoy the fiesta, and four relatives came from La Paz. Two of these, both wife's sisters' husbands gave particularly large presents, demonstrating their success in their new domicile. Alberto's *aini* donors are typical of Compi gift-giving. They indicate both abrupt decrease in relationships with the outside, beyond community boundaries, and also the fact that ties may be extended to distant cities and different ecological areas. Alberto's cash expenditures during the fiesta came to U.S. $39[4]—most of which was spent for enough 90 proof cane alcohol to mix 160 bottles of watered drinks, beer (for the brass band), coca and cigarettes. Furthermore, he used 150 lbs. of his own potatoes, 125 lbs. of *habas*, 100 lbs. of *c'aya*, 100 lbs. of *chuño*, 25 lbs. of barley, and 50 lbs. of dried peas. The total sum of the gifts he received amounted to $31.50 plus 50 lbs. of potatoes, 20 lbs. of *habas*, 12 lbs. of *c'aya*, and 16 lbs. of *oca*. Alberto expected to assume the remaining sponsorship of *preste* of Natividad the following year.

Although Alberto is relatively young the fact that he has sponsored most of the fiestas and has demonstrated his interest in matters concerning ritual and etiquette have placed him high in the prestige hierarchy. On the other hand, the few persons who have not assumed sponsorships may be criticized for the rest of their lives. Roberto, for instance, was called a *yokalla*, or adolescent until he was an old man.

Prestige rating begins early. Today the military service is included in the system. A man named Juan joined because a young man who had just come back from military service taunted him during a fiesta: "You are just a *yokalla* and shouldn't even speak to me: I am as a father unto you because I have fulfilled my obligations." This angered Juan so much that he and his two brothers joined the army soon after, even though he was already married.

Once a person has passed most *cargos* including *preste* of Saint Peter, he is considered to be an elder, or *persona mayor.* He sits in the middle in drinking groups and his opinion carries considerable weight in community gatherings. It is therefore not surprising that the *cargo* system and political influence are closely correlated, even though, contrary to other communities on the altiplano, the fiesta hierarchy and the political hierarchy are not systematically interlinked. For instance, having assumed leadership positions in the community is not a sufficient basis for prestige. A leader's position must be validated by previous or subsequent fiesta sponsorship. Also, fiesta participation is required of all leaders in the sense that at least one section authority should be present at all life crisis celebrations and should sit at the section's site on the plaza during saint's fiestas. On all these occasions he is expected to provide more alcohol than other nonsponsoring participants.

The Fiesta Pattern

The major fiestas in Compi follow the same basic pattern. Usually the sponsorship appointments are made on the day of the fiesta one year in advance when the candidates formally pledge themselves to take over sponsorship obligations. The *preste* of the fiesta of Saint Peter, the largest fiesta, brings candle offerings to the chapel accompanied by his wedding godfather, his *wila maestro* (or master of ceremonies) and a few relatives. The *wila maestro*, who is invariably an older man with experience in feast giving, will aid the *preste* in observing the correct

---

[4] During the same feast, the *cabezas* spent well over $100.00, plus food.

ritual procedures during the fiesta. The sponsors save money for their fiesta for the the entire year preceding the event. Thus Alberto planted onions in almost all his irrigable plots of land, far more than during normal years. He and his wife sold them themselves in La Paz to assure maximum profits. Pablo, another sponsor, purchased llamas and sheep and resold the prepared dried and salted meat to Damaso, a Tauca middleman who sells meat in the Yungas valleys. Lino went to La Paz to work in a glass factory. Faustino found that three months of work in La Paz was insufficient to pay for the costs of the fiesta and that it was necessary to request his brother's financial aid.

Two or three months in advance of the fiesta the sponsors purchase alcohol and coca. At the same time, the *cabeza* organizes the first dance rehearsal with the aid of two or three local musicians. A month or so later another rehearsal takes place. The dancing order is established according to seniority and dancing experience. The *cabeza* hires the band after consulting the dancers, by securing an intermediary or "contractor," a musician from the band's home base. Later the sponsors enlist the help of experienced individuals as cooks, dynamite handlers, waiters and stewards. The latter will take charge of managing the food and alcohol stores. All the helpers and dancers pledge their formal acceptance of their respective functions by accepting half a bottle of watered alcohol bound in a small cloth full of coca (called a *chino*, or bundle) which they then proceed to distribute among the persons present on the occasion the pledge is made.

The fiesta proper begins on the afternoon before the saint's day on the central plaza in front of the church, except on Saint Peter when it begins three days earlier. This formerly permitted each of the three *prestes* to hold a separate mass. Dancing begins. The *altareros* install their tents on the plaza and offer alcohol as well. They and a few followers remain in their respective tents drinking during the entire night. On the saint's day proper the fiesta reaches its climax. Practically the entire community attends and crowds of spectators arrive from neighboring communities, on foot, by bicycle, and by truck. During all fiestas only a few merchants arrive to sell their wares but on Saint Peter's, potters from three or four communities who specialize in this trade stage a large ceramics fair. Although customers arrive in large numbers, especially from nearby islands, few of them stay to watch the fiesta. By the time the dancing begins on the plaza around noon most of the pots have been sold and the clients have departed.

Each section of the community has its own site on the plaza, where the sponsors from its section drink, chew coca, and smoke cigarettes with section officials and elders and where the section dance group performs. Dancing and drinking on the plaza follows a fixed ritual pattern. The disposition of these sites reflects the history and relative prestige of the six sections of Compi-Llamacachi. Compi proper, the original hacienda section, occupies the place of honor in the center of the right side of the plaza. It is the only section whose site is equipped with a stone bench and a stone table. Capilaya, the first section to be added to Compi proper, is found to the right of the latter. The other sections have their sites facing Compi and Capilaya on the left hand side of the plaza with Llamacachi occupying the most marginal position at the lower left.

Throughout the periods of dancing on the plaza the relationships between the sections are enacted symbolically.[5] When the dance groups arrive at the plaza they enter it on their right and dance counterclockwise around it, reaching the site of Compi proper first and that of Llamacachi last. Then only do they move to their own site. During the day each group of dancers and each group of elders must greet all the other groups, again moving counterclockwise from group to group. Each group receives the visitors with cups of alcohol.

On the day after the saint's day, the day of the *preste*, festivities take place beside the compound of the *preste* or *prestes*. On this day the number of *aini* prestations—some of which were already made on previous feast days—grows considerably. Each *aini* is received with three cups of alcohol. The *preste* for the following year and a few relatives and other *ainis* who have pledged to act as his retinue are present as well. Furthermore, each dance group must pay a visit and dance at the *preste's* house for some time. All receive food either from the *preste* himself or from close relatives, such as wife's eldest brother, who feel obligated to provide food as an *aini* prestation. Since for the largest Compi fiesta the triple *preste* sponsorship is assumed by each individual section in turn, the visiting dance groups from each section enhance the link between sections.

The following day is the day of the *cabeza* during which he plays host to his numerous *ainis* and serves the dancers prescribed quantities of meat and other foods which they may take home in recompense for their participation. Contrary to the day of the *preste*, no groups representing other sections appear. All dance in their home section only. This is due to the fact that dance group participation is restricted to the section in which a person lives. Mixed participation in dance groups of other sections is permissible only when the home section fails to organize its own dance group or when two or more sections jointly wish to participate in a fiesta outside of Compi. Otherwise, mixed dance groups mean an incipient switch of allegiance of a part-section to another community section. This is the case in Amasi, a geographically separate part of Compi proper in which the constituent households sometimes organize their own dance group or participate in those of neighboring sections. This reflects other rifts between Amasi and its mother sections. For instance, Amaseños refuse to share the harvest from a plot of former hacienda land located in that area and rarely participate in Compi section meetings.

On the last day of the fiesta, the day of the *servicio*, or helper's day, cooks, stewards, and so on, dance in the patios of the sponsors they have served with all the cooking utensils employed during the fiesta tied to their bodies. The next morning only a few enthusiasts drink in small groups in their homes *curando el ch'aqui*, "to cure their hangover."

Smaller feasts may follow slightly different patterns. During the feast of the Holy Cross the days of the *cabeza* and of the *preste* may coincide when one person assumes the two sponsorships simultaneously. Carnival, New Year's Day, and All

---

[5] Although Compeños are aware of the rules governing symbolic interaction, they are not conscious of the relationship of these rules to their social structure. This relationship reveals itself to the observer only after a thorough analysis of both social and ritual relationships.

Saints' Day are in part celebrated by small groups of relatives in their homes. All Saints' Day is of particular interest since it combines aspects of all fiesta cycles. We shall describe it further on.

Children and Adolescent Fiestas

As we have indicated, adolescents and children participate only marginally during saints' fiestas. They have, however, celebrations of their own. School children celebrate Student's Day and play a minor role in the school anniversary. On both occasions they recite poems, sing hymns, and enact sketches. On Student's Day they also select and crown a school queen following the traditional Hispanic-Latin American pattern introduced by the school teachers, and dance ancient Compi dances at the end. Except on the school anniversary adult community members participate only as spectators.

Adolescent feasts are segregated from the adult world as well. They are not linked to the other fiestas through *aini* prestations and they are staged either at a different time than adult fiestas, at night, or at a different place, on distant sites on the hills rather than in the settled valley bottoms.

KACHUA

The most important adolescent feast is the *kachua*, a sort of "rite of spring" which takes place from November 29th, the beginning of the Aymara calendar until Christmas, the period when the crops begin to grow.

Two or three days before Saint Andrew's (November 29th) two or four dance organizers (a girl and a boy or two girls and two boys), called *kawa iras* who were nominated during the preceding *kachua*, go from house to house announcing the beginning of the celebrations. On the morning of the festivities the male *kawa iras* and a couple of flute players (married men whom the *kawa iras* have asked to participate) call the participants together with their drums. The assembled boys and men climb up the hills surrounding the community, playing their flutes until they reach the traditional *kachua* site, a flat, prominent spot. Each Compi section has its own dance grounds, reflecting the high incidence of section endogamy. On distant hilltops, barely visible to the naked eye, the silhouettes of *kachua* groups from other communities appear (as usual they arrive earlier than the Compeños). The girls join the group an hour later. They bring food including such tidbits as cheese, fried eggs, meat, bread, and fruit. The boys may bring some food of their own plus coca and sweets. Tradition prescribes ritualized food exchange.[6] The principal girl *kawa ira* places part of the food she has brought with her in front of the principal boy *kawa ira*. The action is repeated by the second female *kawa ira* and the rest of the girls follow their leaders' example, placing food on the growing piles in front of the two boy leaders. Boys and girls eat separately, the boys obtaining larger amounts. Later the boys reciprocate with sweets. Then

---

[6] The full ritual is not always implemented. This was the case for the *kachua* we attended, perhaps because the boys were rather young and the group small.

the exchanges are repeated with coca (the cloth with the coca is called the *coca misa*). Finally the girls (in the same order as before) serve alcohol[7] first to the two boy *kawa iras*, then to the flute players and finally to the other boys. Again the boys reciprocate.

Dancing may begin before or after eating and follows distinctive steps. The *kachua* is also one of the few occasions when Aymara sing. The girls always take the initiative in the *kachua* dances. Invariably they know the verses better and in general they tend to be more outgoing and quicker to reply. In contrast the boys act more shy at the beginning. They let the girls stand in a row facing them singing provocative verses such as:

> Brothers, why are you so ashamed?
> We will make you fly like straw, etc.,

while the boys play their flutes feigning indifference for about half an hour. Then only do they approach the girls and begin the dance. At the *kachua* we attended they continued to remain silent while they danced for another half an hour. Then they began to reply to the girls' verses. Each verse sung by them was countered by a barrage of verses sung by the girls. In the first dance figure, boys and girls face each other in two rows and then dance, in a circle, the girls forming one half and the boys the other. Later girls and boys alternate. In the second figure, half the boys and half the girls confront the other half in two chains. Each chain then tries to cut off a part of the other chain. This game goes on until only one person is left in one of the chains or until the dancers tire.

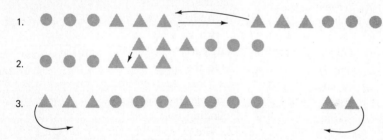

This dance is called the *k'erus wayñusi*. In the last figure, the *wawa wayñusi*, the two mixed chains face each other in the following manner. (Fig. 1)

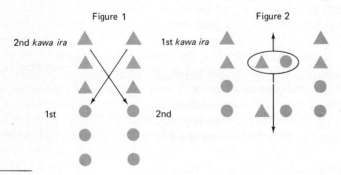

Figure 1   Figure 2

2nd *kawa ira*   1st *kawa ira*

1st   2nd

---

[7] Only very small quantities of alcohol were consumed at the *kachua* we attended.

One pair of *kawa iras* of equal rank hold on to each other and pull one another from one end of the dancing grounds to the other under the arch formed by the other pair until one of the partners falls (Fig. 2). If the male partner falls, the girls sing:

> *Jilata jan ch'amaniquiti, liwtayasi*
> Brother does not have any strength, he has fallen

If the female partner falls, the boys sing:

> *Cullaca . . .*
> Sister . . .

Then the entire group dances down the hill in a snake dance.

The *kachua* may be repeated up to five times on specific dates: Concepción (December 8th), Santa Lucía (December 13th), Santa Barbara (between Santa Lucía and Christmas), and on Christmas. On Christmas the dance takes place on a hill closer to the valley bottom. The food exchanges increase in importance. All the girls, but especially the *kawa iras* attempt to surpass the other by providing more and better food than her rival leader. First they present their two male partners with a plate heaped with potatoes, *oca, uma c'aya* and fish; then another one with *tunta, chuño,* and *tortillas*; a third one with steamed *quinua* dough (*k'espiña*), boiled corn, and cheese, and finally carbonated drinks. The other girls offer their food mixed and do not provide soft drinks. Then the boys reciprocate first with pears, bananas, and bread and then with soft drinks. Of course, the *coca misa* and alcohol is exchanged as well. On this day no special dance figures are observed and no one sings. The *kawa iras* for the following year (sometimes the same persons) are elected as well. Both new and old *kawa iras* are adorned with serpentines. This time the new *kawa iras* lead the snake dance down the hill, followed by the old ones. The dancers descend to the valley between 2:30 P.M. and 3 P.M. instead of at 4–4:30 P.M. as they had done during the other *kachua* dances. They head for the *jilakata's* house where a large number of adults from that section have assembled. Each couple hangs a *huayño* or wreath of bread and fruit around the necks of the *jilakata* and of the magician in charge of preventing hail. The *kawa ira* couples provide two wreaths for each. Then the *jilakata* serves food to all. Dancing continues until sundown.

INTERPRETATION

The *kachua* may be interpreted as a fertility rite (see Chapter 7) in which boys and girls formally enact important social relationships. Contrary to *mestizo* culture, where males are expected to play the most active role in male-female interaction, the boys in the *kachua*, at least initially, play a more passive role than the girls. The latter know the provocative verses best and sing them for a prolonged period of time before the boys even begin to answer. In the end the ritual provides for a show of forces between the two sexes, perhaps to restore the balance of strength between them.

In the *kachua* adolescents also learn some basic ritual patterns, especially the importance of food and alcohol exchange. The dance patterns, at least in larger Compi sections, stress interaction of two groups of actors, a pattern which is present in most dance groups. For instance, panpipes are always played in either identical or complementary pairs; dance groups have two dance leaders, a major and a minor one. Perhaps this reflects the ancient division of Aymara chiefdoms and communities into upper and lower moieties each with its own leader. Although there is no dual organization in Compi today, the double dance groups may nevertheless be seen as a statement of the more generalized Compi sectionalism. Finally, the asymetrical relationship between generations is symbolized in the final scene of the *kachua* when the youngsters pay their respect to the elders by hanging wreaths of bread and fruit around their necks and the elders reciprocate with food.

Crises Rites

Contrary to saints' day fiestas, life crises rites involve a more restricted number of participants including essentially the *ainis* of the person or persons whose rite of passage is being celebrated and the persons who officiate as his ritual godparents during the ceremony. *Ainis* may come from any section of Compi but there are very few persons from outside the community, except at weddings when one of the spouses is a migrant to La Paz or a member of another community. In contrast to saints' feasts all participants bring along their own food and alcohol for distribution in addition to food provided by the sponsors.

The first rite of passage celebrated in Compi families is the *asuti*, described in Chapter 3, which takes place two or three nights after birth. Formerly this rite seems to have been commonly practiced in all Compi sections. Today only Llamacacheños observe it regularly. Contrary to other life crisis rituals, the main actors are children and adolescents. Similar to other adolescent feasts, it takes place at night and *aini* ties are not activated.

Baptism is not accompanied by celebration in Compi. The child is simply inscribed in the civil registry in the *cantón* capital. In contrast, the first haircut a child receives, the *rutucha*, is an important occasion marked by a day of celebrating and gift-giving. This feast takes place at the home of the godparents who sponsor the feast jointly with the parents of the child. It begins with a meal of all participants, the *ainis* of the godparents and the *ainis* of the parents eating in separate groups, followed by a ritual exchange of coca and alcohol between the two groups of *ainis*. The godmother and the mother and the godfather and the father must serve each other constantly until they are completely inebriated. Then, following the godfather's example, the constituents of the godfather and some of the father's group place money on a plate full of crop samples, cut a lock of the child's hair, place it into the plate, and kiss the crop samples. All the others crowd around them each offering a small cupful of alcohol, part of which the *ainis* sprinkle on the plate and part of which they drink themselves. This practice ensures future prosperity of the child. Then the process is repeated with another plate representing the child's father. At the end the money given as *aini* to the godfather and the father is counted. The community leaders call all participants in turn, beginning with the sponsors and the elders and ending with the young members, to kiss the money and drink alcohol once more. Subsequently, all dance to the tune of a brass band wearing clothing provided by the godfather's household.

The *rutucha* is typical of large family feasts. The groups involved are primarily made up of the personal and familial ties of the main actors. They consist of relatives, friends and persons who wish to secure or reciprocate for a following for their own feasts. Nevertheless the obligatory presence of a section leader may be seen as a statement that the ceremony concerns not only the main actors but the section to which they belong as a whole. This fact is of special significance when the godparents and parents belong to different sections. In such cases the presence of leaders from two sections indicates the fact that social interaction between members of different sections creates bonds not only between two couples but between the two sections to which they belong.

The homecoming from the year-long military service is the next rite of passage observed in Compi. This practice seems to be a carry-over from colonial times when *comunidad* members returning from forced labor in the silver mines of Potosí were feasted on their arrival, as well as from an ancient hacienda practice of feasting persons who had served the patrón selling produce in his store in La Paz. A large proportion of the young man's section members greet him when his truck arrives and offer him food which he redistributes among his friends and followers. Later drinking continues at his home in a smaller group.

Marriage marks full attainment of adult status and is therefore the most important rite of passage. Celebrations last for three consecutive days. Like the haircutting ceremony the wedding takes the form of a number of ritual meals, libations, and the presentation of *aini* gifts by the relatives and other *ainis* of the spouses' parents and of the godparents selected by the bride's parents as mediators in case of marriage disputes. They arrive singly or in small groups and are received by the couple and godparents. An older man, the *taka padrino*, sees to it that the couple and godparents observe the proper greetings. Again the fertility and prosperity of the married couple are ensured by a ceremony resembling the blessing of crop samples, *atarutucha*. At the end of the celebration the elders ritually admonish the couple not to "sell the honor of the community and that of the marriage godfather."

The social significance of the wedding rituals closely parallels that of the *rutucha*. The main difference lies in the greater importance attached to the wedding, the larger number of participants, and the fact that presentations are made to the bride and groom and not to the godparents.

The next rite of passage takes place one, two, or three years after the wedding when the couple builds their first house, usually on one of the husband's father's plots of land. This ceremony ritually states the relationship between the couple and their parents and their newly-acquired status of household heads. Traditionally, the husband's father provides the poles for the front part of the roof and the wife's father for the back, considered to be respectively the right hand side and the left hand side of the house. The roofing proper is usually accomplished in a single day in a large work bee. Toward evening, when the roof is finished, other *acompañantes*, relatives, friends, and neighbors appear to celebrate the *achokalla* or *utachiri* ceremony. All bring cooked food with them, some baskets full of flowers to hang from the rafters outside (a La Paz custom), and some *aini* presentations in the form of a bottle or two of alcohol, cigarettes, or larger quantities of food. As a first act, the father of the houseowner provides two *chinos* for the builders for the "right hand side" of the house, the father-in-law for the "left." The bottles are rolled down the roof slopes, caught as they fall, and hung up on the rafters by their necks. Then the section magician offers a burnt offering of sweets and the fat of pigs, llamas and cows to the *condor mamani*, or spirit of the house. After eating and drinking, the participants whip each other ritually with the dangling ends of a rope hung from the rafters. Some also sing songs deploring the defaults of their partners. This practice is paralleled by a similar act in the *asuti* ceremony in which the adolescents hit the hands of the spectators accusing them of various misdeeds such as beating their wives when inebriated. Perhaps, as William Carter has suggested, this ceremony serves to clear the atmosphere of latent hostilities thus assuring the couple and their relatives of a future unburdened by past tension. Dancing continues until the next morning when both the father and the father-in-law of the houseowner sacrifice a sheep to the spirit of the house. The meat is divided among the helpers.

What seems so important in the *utachiri* ceremony is not primarily the construction of a house as such but the establishment of a new household. This can

Couple and compadres *greeting* ainis *at their wedding.*

be deduced from the fact that when a house replaces a former structure which had been built on the same site, no sheep sacrifice is necessary.

The next and last rituals accorded to an individual are a series of death ceremonies beginning with those surrounding the burial and ending with the All Saints' rituals. Compeños inter the deceased on the day following death. A female relative living in the same compound announces the death by running around the house, her head covered with a black cloth wailing and lamenting. Relatives and neighbors visit her during that night holding vigil. The next morning a carpenter will make a coffin, others wash the cadaver, dress it, and place it into the coffin. A relative or ritual kin begins cooking food for a large number of kin and other community members who arrive around noon, the women laden with cooking pots filled with soup. If the deceased was a respected elder or the wife of such an elder, almost every household in the section plus those of his relatives from other sections will be represented at this ceremonial meal. The men wear everyday clothing while most women carry black shawls. They offer plates of soup to the closest male relatives of the deceased, for example, to the eldest living son, the father, or the husband, who directs the ritual activities and provides a large proportion of the food. He redistributes them by means of his *servicio*. The latter also spreads food on cloths in front of the mourners. The elders, sitting near the master of ceremonies, comment on the merits of the deceased. After all have eaten their fill, the rest of the food is distributed among the participants. Then the men carry the coffin to the cemetery while the women leave their empty pots and the food they have received at home. All bring alcohol along.

The Compi cemetery is rather badly kept. Small dirt huts constructed over the graves lie spread in a jumbled and at first sight completely haphazard manner over a centrally located hilltop. Nevertheless, each section of the community, including Llamacachi, has its separate burial grounds and its site where the elders assemble. Also, where space permits, relatives tend to be buried in close proximity to each other.

The master of ceremonies and the elders sit down at the site allocated to their section and all place their coca bundles or *taris*, in front of him. When the women arrive, they likewise sit in a group around the master of ceremony's wife or other close relative. While the two groups indulge in ritual libations, a group of young men dig the grave.

Drinking is heavy, for not only does every person bring his own alcohol but the master of ceremonies provides ten quarts or so of his own. The coffin is lowered into the ground and all help to shovel earth onto it. By this time the sun has set. Most participants disperse and only some close relatives and ritual kin accompany the master of ceremonies to the deceased's home. There, kneeling on the floor, each prays for the deceased. While some men chat or quarrel, most sleep in uncomfortable positions on a bed or in a corner. What happens during the first vigil after a person's death is of particular significance to the community. At a vigil one of the authors attended, a thunderstorm struck in the middle of the night. The *jilakata* took a bottle of alcohol and made signs with it and his index finger to prevent hail. All were relieved when no hail fell for this could have meant a bad harvest. The next evening a smaller group of relatives renews their vigil repeating this once more on the following evening. Eight days after the funeral (or sometimes earlier) a ceremony is held to announce the definite departure of the deceased's soul. The men assemble at the house of the deceased person and are followed by the women bringing food. Again they comment on the deceased and on the plight of the bereaved members of his family. Then all kneel in front of a cross standing on a black carrying cloth which belonged to the deceased. A person who knows how to recite prays a series of Catholic prayers which are repeated by the participants. Then the *servicios* spread lengths of cloth on the ground and food provided by the master of ceremonies on it. Again one eats as at the funeral. However, this time, fruit, bread, and llamas, which are made out of *k'espiña* to carry the food offerings to the land of the dead are served as well. Again the remaining food is divided among the participants after setting aside a large portion for the person who recited the prayers and for the secretary-general or other higher official representing the community at the feast. All chew coca and smoke cigarettes provided by the master of ceremonies and some of his relatives. The entire ceremony lasts only about three hours.

Except for those families who have a mass read for the deceased (usually one month after their death) the deceased's relatives remember him only at All Saints'.

In addition to these life crisis feasts, some Compeños celebrate the day of the *compadre*, when the marriage godchild should visit his godparents loaded with food and accompanied by a few followers. Some Compeños, especially younger ones, also celebrate their birthdays by inviting a few friends and relatives to drink at their homes. Finally, ceremonies are conducted when a calamity, such as the advent of twins, the death of an animal or human being by lightning, and so on, occurs; these are attended by many people, primarily those from the sponsor's sections. We shall describe such ceremonies under the heading of magic.

All Saints'

We have reserved the description of All Saints' to the end since it occupies a peculiar position in the ritual cycle of the community. It contains elements both particular to life-crisis rites, for it is held in commemoration of deceased family members, as well as communal elements, since it synchronizes these family devotions in a single feast in which the entire community participates. Thus it constitutes the counterpart of the fiesta system for the realm of the dead, a replica of the main characteristics of the fiestas for the living concentrated in a three-day period for the dead.

Essentially All Saints' consists of the preparation of banquets for the dead, especially by the families in which a death has occurred within the last three to five years, and the distribution of this food among relatives and other persons who come to pray for the deceased, first in the homes and later in the cemetery. The celebrations end with dancing on the plaza.

The principal figures during the feast are the *chhamaka prestes* (literally, "*prestes* of darkness," sponsors of the dead). The *chhamaka preste* is either the father or the eldest son of the deceased. When these relatives are not living any longer, or if the deceased had no sons, the son-in-law, or in the last instance the oldest living brother, the wife's second husband, or the eldest male relative with whom the deceased shared a compound take over the duties of *chhamaka preste*. In all instances he must be male. He (or in subsequent years often his close relatives) is responsible for the preparation and provision of most of the specified foods to be offered to the deceased's soul. This includes bread shaped into wreaths (representing flower wreaths), ladders (for the souls to climb out of purgatory), old men and babies (symbolizing the souls of old persons and of infants respectively), and animals, such as llamas (standing for the deceased's herd) baked in ovens which are rarely used during the rest of the year;[8] figures are formed out of *quinua* dough by the *chhamaka preste's* close relatives and steamed in a pot to carry the food offerings to the land of the dead, which lies far off in the west. There are dogs to help the soul herd the llamas, reed boats to carry the soul across the lake, and so on; onions with enlarged stalks represent the deceased's drinking vessels; sugar cane is the deceased's walking stick. Also included are fruit, coca and alcohol if the deceased was an adult, and milk if he was an infant.

Not only relatives, friends and neighbors, but boys, old bachelors, and widows as well, make their way from house to house praying and singing certain Catholic prayers and filling their baskets with food (including the steamed figures) in the process. Praying in the home lasts for the entire afternoon, the night, and part of the next morning. Praying and food distribution in the cemetery lasts for little more than an hour with almost the entire community present.

The dancing on the plaza which follows the ceremony in the cemetery is quite different from other fiestas. The *chhamaka prestes* take the place of the *prestes* in normal feasts, drinking with the elders on the section sites. The dance groups are composed mainly of boys, girls, and young men. The young boys, clothed in ancient ponchos, wearing masks, and carrying crooked staffs represent old men. Older boys and young men are dressed in skirts which once belonged to deceased women. Their faces hidden behind black *lijjllas* (shawls) they mimic indecent female behavior. The girls are in their Sunday best and carry dolls and even babies borrowed from their adult sisters, a practice supposed to insure fertility in their later married life. Thus dance participation reverses the roles acted in normal life. Role reversal is practiced in many societies to indicate that the ritual activities being carried out belong to a different sphere than everyday life. In this case the dancers represent the dead, and not living section members as they do in other fiestas. The burlesque character of these dances counterbalances the serious previous acts. Snake dances in which many of the spectators and elders take part also contribute to a more relaxed atmosphere. Like the sponsors in normal feasts, the *chhamaka prestes* are accompanied to their homes by a group of followers, mainly elders, who drink there for some time before they move to the home of another *chhamaka preste*. This communal aspect of the fiesta lasts till the evening of the next day.

---

[8] Compeños did not make bread traditionally and purchase all their bread in local stores or on the market at present.

Todos Santos combines elements of small family rituals (the home cele-brations of families with no recent deaths), large family rituals (those of *chhamaka prestes*) and community celebrations in one fiesta. During the first day, family rituals are merely coordinated but held separately by each family, the after-noon of the second day all ritual activities are concentrated on one site, the ceme-tery, without losing their familial character. Finally toward the evening, the cele-brations become communal on the plaza. The link between family and community ritual is established by the fact that *chhamaka prestes* are treated like sponsors of major fiestas in spite of the familial nature of their role, and by groups of flute players, children, poor widows, and so on, who go from house to house playing, singing, and reciting prayers during the familial part of the feast.

Sex and Death Symbolism in *Todos Santos* and the *Asuti*

In significant ways Todos Santos resembles the *asuti*, or child birth ritual (*cf.* Chapter 3). Both deal with sexuality and death. But the meaning attached to these themes is diametrically opposed due to the fact that the *asuti* marks the beginning of the life cycle while All Saints' reflects upon life after death. The *asuti* deals with sexual vigor among living human beings represented by children acting animal roles. All Saints' deals with sexual excess or misplaced sexual behavior among souls represented by persons acting roles inverting sex. In the *asuti*, death is seen as an act of theft by the condor, a scavenger who is mocked because he smells of putrefaction. Comic relief is assured by representing the parents of the stolen child as oldsters who should no longer reproduce. All Saints' sees in death the possibility of the continuation or renewal of life. Nubile girls carry dolls or their sisters' babies around to assure their own fertility. Comic relief is provided by representing the souls by actors in age groups with the lowest mortality rate.

Extra-Community Fiestas

Compeños also visit a number of fiestas in neighboring communities. They do not, however, participate as sponsors and rarely as *ainis*. While the sponsors usually do not serve alcohol to strangers, their friends and relatives from other communities do receive occasional drinks and may even participate actively in the celebrations. Nicolás, for instance, a Compeño whose wife comes from neighbor-ing Chua, loads his donkey with alcohol, produce, and bedding and stays over at his father-in-law's house during the major fiesta in Chua. Men and women from other communities watch the dancers in segregated groups. Friends and relatives, especially younger men, also drink in small groups, each person purchasing two bottles of regular beer made in La Paz or home-brewed maize beer from one of the vendors. Until recently a Compi dance group also participated in the feast of Candlemas (February 2d) in Jank'o Amaya. The reason given for their participa-tion was to enlist the aid of the miraculous virgin of Jank'o Amaya against ill-ness. However, participation in this feast also reflected social factors. Only rich persons could afford the expensive costumes required for the feast, for these had to be owned outright by the dancers and could not be rented. First, members from the original hacienda section, Compi proper, and later a mixed dance group from the three largest sections participated, thus representing the combined elite of the community.

County seats celebrate feasts of their own. Previous to the agrarian reform, the *jilakatas* of Llamacachi and other free communities (but not ex-haciendas) belonging to the county of Santiago de Huata each had the obligation to sponsor a dance group from his community for the feast of the county seat's patron saint, a feast which included both Indian and *mestizo prestes*.

Presently both Compi and Llamacachi organize dance groups to participate in the New Year's feast which marks the end of the county official's term in office. Dance groups are invited from all the member communities. However, in practice only those communities organize dance groups who have furnished an official during the previous year or who will do so the coming year. *Cantón* authorities who are from Compi are accompanied by combined or separate dance groups from most Compi sections—flute players or brass bands depending on means and the importance given to the occasion.

In Jank'o Amaya each member community has its site where authorities and their retinue drink and dance. In contrast to participation in New Year's celebrations, the annual bullfight in Jank'o Amaya, an institution every self-respecting county seat must observe, entails the participation of most member communities as well as that of groups of vendors selling the same produce in the local fair and the truckers who provide transportation. Each section pays for a number of rounds and for the money-laden cloths which are tied to the bulls. The cloths will be torn

Bicycle race during a regional folklore festival in Compi.

off by courageous participants. This feast also has the largest dance group composed of migrants to La Paz the authors have observed at any fiesta.

Nevertheless this feast is still primarily a community affair. Dance groups are composed entirely of community members, the largest dance group being organized by migrants from Jank'o Amaya to La Paz. The county capital must provide for some representation of its member communities and of the market network. This it fulfills by means of the bullfight. However, like all other county institutions, the feast serves its own interests prior to those of other communities who belong to the county. In this respect the main difference between the Jank'o Amaya fiesta and those of communities which are not county capitals, lies in the size and prestige of the feast which in turn attracts a larger number of migrants.

In addition to the feasts described above, Compeños participate in a series of celebrations of a much vaster scale which have sprung up in recent years. These are the folklore festivals whose origin lies in the efforts of the M.N.R. regime to uphold Indian customs by showing traditional dances on national holidays in the La Paz soccer stadium. More recently such festivals have been held in the country as well, where they have attracted large crowds of Pazeños and foreign tourists. In 1965, Compi became the site of one of the largest annual festivals organized by the Bolivian tourist service and numerous Compeños, among whom returned migrants played a major role. In 1967, dance groups from all over the altiplano participated. The festival also featured an exposition of agricultural produce and handicrafts, the coronation of a beauty queen, a bicycle race for Compi and Llamacachi girls, and a reed boat race for all surrounding communities. The folklore festivals are thus an interesting mixture of past and present Aymara as well as *mestizo* customs. The dances must be traditional ones accompanied by reed instruments rather than by brass bands. Many ancient dances have been revived in order to win the prizes donated to the best groups. In the exposition new varieties of crops introduced by development agencies are shown together with established ones. The coronation of a beauty queen is, of course, a hispanic custom. Female bicycling was introduced in Compi only in 1966 and has experienced a rapid upsurge due to the advantageous economic position of young Compi girls discussed earlier, while reed boats are a traditional element and are being replaced increasingly by larger wooden ones. Apart from the Compi festival, others are held in the Cochabamba valley where the agrarian reform laws were originally signed. Recently, Aymara radio announcers in La Paz have organized a series of these festivals in open theaters in La Paz, and Compeños have participated in both. Like the Compi festival they reflect the increasing efforts of Bolivian officials on the one hand and migrants on the other to give the peasants a national identity and to have Aymara and Quechua folklore accepted as part of the national heritage.

Limits of Participation

Almost all Compeños are involved in the fiesta system in one way or the other, for even those individuals or groups who wish to remain aloof from it cannot entirely escape its influence. Most migrants participate in, or at least attend, feasts

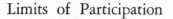

either in Compi, or in La Paz, or in both places. Two or three migrants who have returned to Compi refuse to spend their own resources in fiestas but are nevertheless among the principal organizers of the Compi festival and of dance groups which participate in La Paz theaters. Older bachelors may not act as sponsors, but nevertheless participate as *dispenseros*.

The case of the Protestants is more complicated. In theory they should not drink alcohol at all, although the Baptists at least are allowed to attend fiestas. When they cannot refuse to participate actively in such feasts as weddings, or *rutuchas* where one of the spouses or one of the parents is a Protestant, they bring bottles of soft drinks instead of alcohol. Considerable tension prevails during such mixed fiestas. A Protestant godfather may be forced to drink in the end while all Protestants who refuse to drink are sharply criticized and ridiculed. Members of the Pentecostal sect are not allowed to attend fiestas at all, nor can they attend soccer matches. A young man who had recently converted to this sect had to defend himself against a group of drunken Compeños who went to his house during a fiesta and challenged him to a fistfight. When one of the assailants was hurt, resentment mounted against the Protestant for it is considered extremely inappropriate for a sober person to fight with an inebriated one.

In order to alleviate the pressures on their congregation and give them a sense of group identity, the Baptist mission has introduced large gatherings in which Protestants from the entire area participate in prayers, confessions, discussion groups, singing, and so on. These are held annually during Easter week. In 1965, a large gathering also took place during All Saints', followed a few weeks later by a procession in La Paz which included Protestants from all over the country. Thus what could be considered as a rival ritual cycle with participants from a much wider area than that encompassed by traditional feasts may be developing among the Protestants.

*

*   *

Compi fiestas appear on the one hand as a system with rules of its own based on a combination of elements: precolumbian agricultural and life-crises rites, and what is probably an essentially indigenous reciprocity system (*aini* gift giving); Roman Catholic saints' days and baptism, marriage, and death practices; and syncretic costumed dancing patterns and sponsorship obligations. On the other hand, it may be seen as the reflection of the social organization. Most anthropologists have stressed the aspect of fiestas as a separate institution with functions of its own. Thus some authors have seen in the fiesta system a means of redistribution of wealth (Carter, 1964) and even of economic levelling (Nash, 1958). Others have seen it as a means of producing social stratification by elevating all sponsors to a higher social category (Cancian, 1965), or as an adjunct to local annual fairs geared to attracting clients. Still others have seen it as a means by which the Catholic Church and *mestizo* beverage vendors and creditors could siphon economic surplus from Indian communities (Harris, 1964).[9] It is our opinion that all these functions, as important as they may be, are not sufficient to explain either the persistence of the fiesta complex under a great variety of contexts in the face of sweeping social change, nor the richness of its forms. Rather, we would see in it an important means of communicating both continuity and change in social relationships. It furnishes a symbolic system which in the Bolivian highlands is common to peasant communities, towns, and cities in which both internal social differentiation and/or integration and ties in farflung networks of interpersonal ties can be expressed.

---

[9] In some parts of Ecuador church revenues are still strongly connected with fiestas. In Bolivia this is no longer true, for the church has lost its importance as a political force.

7

Religion

IN THIS CHAPTER we intend to explore the relationship between Aymara mental constructs of the natural and supernatural realms and their social structure. We will then elucidate some of the principles which govern Aymara operations of thought. Ritual will then be seen as a bridge or media between social structure and cognitive principles. Finally, we shall analyze the role of the magician and curer in Aymara society.

The Aymara of Compi/Llamacachi distinguish between the spheres of nature and the supernatural. These spheres are seen in a relationship of interdependence or mutuality rather than causality. Thus an event in a human life, especially an atypical one, is reflected in the state of nature. Explanations of phenomena occurring in the domain of human life are explained in terms of phenomena in the natural and supernatural realms and vice versa.

The Social Origins of Aymara Thought

First we shall examine the social origins of Aymara thought. For Compeños nature includes plants, animals, topographical features, the weather and human beings. This preoccupation with nature is evident in daily conversation, in formal and informal education, in community meetings and in feasts such as the *asuti*.

Compeños are not only preoccupied with nature, they observe and classify it according to minute differences. For instance the potato, the main staple, is classified on the basis of the following features: shape (one potato is called cow's tongue); size (large or small ones of a particular type); and color (black, red, spotted). In one particular field we were shown twenty different varieties, each with its own physical characteristics which served to distinguish its use in cooking or storage.

Animals such as sheep are recognized by herders on the basis of genealogy, size, type of wool, and so on. In addition, each site in the village, as a matter of fact almost every plot and every topographical feature in the hills, is named. For example, one field is known as the Place of Ovens, because once upon a time an oven was found there. In the same way Compeños specify type of wind and clouds according to origin and kind, among other things. This classification of plants, animals and topographical features is directly related to the agricultural herding and marketing activities discussed in Chapter 2.

In the Aymara world view there is also a supernatural sphere. This can be considered distinct because, as we shall show later, parallelisms are revealed between the supernatural and nature but not within the supernatural. But since the Aymara in Compi and Llamacachi are not given to abstract philosophical speculations, they classify supernaturals in very much the same way that they distinguish natural phenomena. Most of the supernaturals are placebound. For instance, the midwife asks the coca the location of the spirit where one should give offerings in order to facilitate birth. *Pachamama* is the Earth Mother. The *achachilas* are lake and mountain spirits. *Rayos* or lightning is worshiped at the site where lightning has struck. *Anchanchus* are evil place spirits usually associated with caves. Other supernaturals are actual persons, such as the *Karisiris*, who rob children of their fat during sleep. (There are supposed to be persons in the community who do such strange things.) Similarly those *yatiris* or curers who perform black magic are supposed to possess supernatural powers. In the stories told to children and by children, animals are added to place spirits and humans. These include the Condor, Tiwula (the fox), the Skunk and the Duck. These animal supernaturals are described with actual animal characteristics (for example, the duck swims).

It is not difficult to locate the social origins of these supernaturals. *Pachamama*, for example, has her origins in the mother figure. Just as the relation between coitus and conception is fully understood, so is the relation of the earth (*Pachamama*) and lifegiving plants and animals. This is expressed symbolically by the fact that one libates alcohol to the "Earth" during feasts. Just as human mothers are unpredictable so is *Pachamama*. The social importance of fertility may be further emphasized in the role of children in the community. Most of the political assemblies concern the school and important feasts, such as All Saints', take account of children.

We have seen how two modes of thought, the natural and supernatural classifications, find their origins in the economic and socio-political sub-structures. At this point, it is incumbent upon us to present the implicit principles which determine Aymara folk taxonomy.

Principles of Aymara Folk Taxonomy

Within the realm of nature, the Aymara make a distinction between humans on the one hand and plants, animals, topographical features and the weather on the other hand. This distinction becomes evident when we note that the Aymara use parallelisms between these two categories but not *within* each category. Like the classifications and other distinctions, these parallelisms between the human sphere and the sphere of plants, animals, etc., seem to be based on minute distinctions in texture, action, state and sex.

Field research revealed the following parallelisms based on texture. In one of the prenatal precautions, the mother is not supposed to handle wool; a hairy child upon birth is related to the handling of wool, on the part of the mother. A similar relationship is displayed in the taboo which should be observed in the presence of an infant. One may not toast maize or broad beans.. The wish for the navel cord to dry is related to toasted plants. Furthermore, a child's first teeth are placed in either *sewenka*, a type of sedge grass with sharp edges, or in a rat's hole. The sawlike edges of the grass and the small sharp teeth of the rat are comparable to the child's teeth. Another parallelism based on texture may be found in the treatment for scarlet fever; one is supposed to grind up stone from a special hill and put it on the skin of the child. The eruptions on the skin are similar to the face of this particular hill. Grinding up stone from this hill is then like dissolving the infected skin of the child.

Parallelisms between the human and natural worlds are expressed in terms of similarity of action as well. The treatment of pregnant women and sheep is similar. One does not enrage them. Moreover, the winding of yarn, prior to the birth of a child, is associated with a twisted umbilical cord. The taboo on weaving near a newborn child, an activity requiring a pulling *out* action, may be inversely related to the hope that the umbilical cord may remain tucked *in*. Breastfeeding is also related to nature. A nursing mother should not come too near incense which is made from the dried sap of a tree. The dried sap is directly related to the drying up of the life-preserving milk. In addition, the flow of blood from cutting the tongue with *sewenka* may correspond to the flow of words, that is, speech in a previously mute child. In the same way the whirring of the wings of a dragon-fly may be related to the movement of the tongue in speech. Similarly, the killing of a snake, one of the crawling creatures, is thought to be associated with the child's inability to crawl.

The Aymara seem to base parallelisms not only on texture and action but on a similar state or condition as well. For example, a pregnant woman is supposed to work in the fields to ensure the fertility of the fields as well as her own fertility, but a menstruating woman may not go into the fields. Menstruation, the negation of fertility in women, is related to unproductive fields. Infertility in humans and in animals is one and the same thing. A barren woman is known as a mule. Moreover infertility caused by a voluntary or involuntary act of abortion is accompanied by unusual states of nature: hail or ferocious winds.

Abortions are discouraged and lamented by the family and the community alike. The woman's family is concerned, alarmed and angered by this transgression, for "what will the people say?" The authorities, the *alcalde*, the official responsible for agricultural rites, and the magician responsible for imploring the spirits to keep away the hail put pressure on the woman to confess. It is said that in the neighboring community, when hail falls, the officials feel the breasts of all the unmarried girls to see if they contain milk which can be, of course, indicative of recent pregnancy. For if hail should fall, the blame rests on her if she has not disposed of the aborted fetus in the prescribed manner. Abortions are considered "una pena para la comunidad." Since this expression was used with some frequency, we think it should be explained at this point. Any transgression of the natural flow of events was considered an affliction or grief-bringing act involving suffering for the person in question and for the community as well.

To prevent the catastrophe of hail, which might ruin the fields completely, one must dispatch and bury, or dispose of, the aborted fetus on one of the two highest mountains in the vicinity of the community.

A sense of reality may be conveyed by the following incident: on August 25, 1965, Juana the wife of Pascual, gave "birth" to cells that had never formed a fetus, a hydromole. This occurrence was treated in the manner prescribed for abortions. The *Yatiris* gave *mesas* or burnt offering consisting of sweets, *kantutas* (unidentified) the national flower, fats, incense, seeds, nuts, shells, herbs, and scraped stones which were presented to the *achachilas* or spirits of the different mountains. In this case Pascual spent 300 pesos bolivianos or 25 American dollars for a *Chhiuchhi mesa*. *Chhuichhi* (meaning chicks) *mesa* is one in which miniature lead figures are offered to the *achachilas* (spirits) of the hills. Each hill possesses its named spirit, most of which are male. These *achachilas* are ranged in a hierarchy of importance. In this case the *mesa* was offered to Jipi. Jipi is the name both of the highest Andean foothill east of Compi and the name of the spirit of the mountain.[1]

The adolescent rite of the *kachua* reveals the parallelism based on similarity of condition extremely well. As we have mentioned, a girl and boy are chosen to act as hosts and leaders. These two are called the mother and father of the *kachua*. After a dance in which they tease each other, they perform a mock marriage which reduplicates all the sequences and personages necessary for an actual wedding. The *kachua* songs mention fruits and flowers in each refrain. One reason given for holding the *kachua* is that then "the flowers bloom for joy." Thus the fertility of the adolescents symbolized by the mock wedding is associated with the blooming of flowers.

Parallelisms between the two spheres is also expressed in terms of sex. The midwife "reads in the coca," divines, to predict the sex of the child to be born: the leaves that are rounder than usual denote a female; lanceolate ones a male. In the case of twins the foregoing parallelism is expressed in this manner: "a pair of boys is like *habas* (broad beans), wheat and barley; a pair of girls bespeaks a harvest of potatoes and *oca*." (Male and female crops respectively).

The foregoing parallelisms of the human and natural spheres represent more than merely the identity or association of unequal elements. What is related are not so much *characteristics* but *similar relationships*. For instance, abortion is related to normal birth as hail is related to propitious climatic conditions. Abortion does not cause hail, nor does normal birth cause fertile fields, but in order to attain balance in the forces of nature a complementary normality in human reproduction must be maintained.

---

[1] The fetus was buried on Jipi, the sacred hill, by the *mayores*, or elders (anyone who has the courage may do so). A few days later when Juana hemorrhaged, the blood also had to be disposed of ritually. A person carrying an aborted fetus is considered particularly vulnerable for noxious winds in the hills, the so-called *Limpu*, carry illness and suffering. The same rite is performed when children die before being named.

Manipulating the Supernatural

The Aymara attempt to balance the nature/human equilibrium by the judicious manipulation of the supernatural. This balancing manifests itself in certain feasts as well as in magical practices.

Any community member may contribute to the manipulation of the supernatural but often specialists must be called. These belong to two categories, old persons who know how to recite Catholic prayers and fragments of the cathechism and curer/magicians. The former are called for funerals, masses for the dead, All Saints', and the twin ceremony which we shall describe later. They recite prayers as well as direct religious chants. The latter specialists, called *yatiris* or *maestros*, are held in particularly high esteem in the community. As we have mentioned, their opinion carries considerable weight in assemblies. Their position is acknowledged ritually in such ceremonies as the *kachua* when wreaths of bread are placed around their necks. Their prestige is due to the fact that they are indispensable as intermediaries between nature and the supernatural, a role which they enact vis-à-vis individual community members as well as the section to which they belong as a whole.

For personal services which include curing, divining, and sorcery, the aid of a range of persons from both inside and outside the community may be enlisted. Some of these individuals merely profess a knowledge of the medicinal properties of herbs, others are midwives, and still others divine with the aid of coca leaves. Only a handful are full-fledged magicians capable of officiating in rites for the section as a whole and of these, usually only one in each section is called upon to serve his section. These few individuals may hold such positions for many years. As a remuneration for their services they receive prepared food, alcohol, and coca.

MAGICIANS

Not everybody is considered capable of becoming a magician. Aymara magicians frequently claim that they had been struck by lightning and thus knew that they had been singled out by the spirits to become magicians. Quintin, a Capilaya magician, attributed his decision to become a magician to a prolonged illness. He became a *maestro* when he was well in his forties. He had been living in La Paz for ten years and had become ill. After entering a hospital his health improved somewhat. Soon afterwards his *compadre*, a *maestro* who could "read the coca" revealed to him that his illness was caused by supernatural forces, a sign that he should become *a maestro*, too. Quintin then returned to Compi and asked a *yatiri* from Jank'o Amaya to help him request the Achachila of Kakape, a Compi mountain, to give him permission to practice magic. During part of the trip up the hill Quintin rode on a donkey, still feeling too weak from his illness to walk; halfway up he suddenly felt better and was able to proceed on foot. He claims that from that moment on there has been no illness in his family. On top of Kakape the initiation took place with a sacrifice to the mountain's *achachila*. Later the wife of another *yatiri* suggested that Quintin affirm his position as *maestro* by making a pilgrimage to Oje, a community whose patron saint, an image of Saint Peter, is considered to be endowed with miraculous powers. Favorable circumstances, however, elevated Quintin to the position of section magician that very same year and thus the trip to Oje became unnecessary. In previous years there had been no magicians in Capilaya. Feliciano, a Compeño who was at the same time *sot'a*, or chief aide to the *mayordome* of the hacienda, an administrator hated in the community because of the unpopular measures he had introduced in Compi to gain the favor of the patrón, acted as magician of both Compi proper and Capilaya. The year Quintin became a magician the harvest in Capilaya had been bad because hail had fallen in that section alone, sparing the rest of the hacienda. This was attributed to Feliciano's disinterest in a section to which he did not belong. Thus the Capilaya *colonos* asked Quintin to direct the important hail ceremonies. According to the magician, the crops produced abundantly again during subsequent years forcing even the patrón to recognize him as section magician in spite of the intrigues of Feliciano.

Apart from the process of becoming a magician, Quintin's case also illustrates how modern medicine (represented by the La Paz hospital), Catholicism (the desirability of the magicians' endorsement by the image of Saint Peter in Oje), and magic are not considered to be incompatible but instead have complementary or reinforcing functions in an individual's life. Saint Peter may be called upon like any powerful mountain spirit to bestow magical powers on an individual. The fact that Quintin's health improved in the hospital did not lead him to doubt his *compadre's* verdict that supernatural forces had brought about his illness. Quintin's story also exemplifies both section rivalries and the relationship with overseers appointed by the patrón. Capilaya considered itself to be at a disadvantage vis-à-vis other sections because it did not have its own magician. The resentment against the Compi magician's unfavorable activities as a *sot'a* enhanced these rivalries.

SACRIFICE, EXCHANGE, AND MEDIATION

Section magicians are busy men, especially during the growing season. One of the main recurrent tasks a magician faces is making incantations and preparing offerings to combat hail. On certain days of the year and when there is imminent danger of hail during the crucial periods of the agricultural cycle (January through April), the *jilakata* calls the section magician and a few aides to his home. The magicians begins the propitation of the spirits by preparing four cups of alcohol and placing three coca leaves in each as a first offering to the spirits. The first two he throws to the west and to the east, the second pair to the south and to the north. Then all prepare an offering of herbs (*juira k'oa*), fat (pig's fat for the lake spirits or llama fat for the mountain spirits [pigs are frequently driven to the lake while llamas usually remain on the hill flanks] depending on whether the hail is expected from the direction of the lake or from the direction of the hills), cotton, wool, and a small piece of wildcat fur. When all is prepared the helpers, men with experience in preparing and presenting offerings, climb up on the main hills around Compi to burn these offerings, murmuring incantations to the *achachilas* to protect their fields. Acting as a magical assistant is considered to be fraught with danger. For instance, Alberto's epileptic seizures are sometimes attributed to his functions as an assistant to the *maestros*. The people say that perhaps he had forgotten some important ingredient in the offering, thereby conjuring the wrath of the *achachilas*. And yet Alberto must continue with these activities for the spirits are used to him and are more likely to accept offerings from him than from some novice.

While the helpers are away the magician prepares and presents offerings to be given at a prominent spot in the valley, an ancient precolumbian grave believed to belong to a "heathen." At the same time the *jilakata* and all the community members burn straw in their patios to chase the hail away and implore the *achachilas* to protect them. Divining from the way coca leaves fall on a cloth, the magician prognosticates whether the aides will be successful and their sacrifice accepted by the *achachilas*, whether magicians from other communities are sending hail over to their valley, and so on. Finally the helpers return from the hills and recount their success or attempt to explain their failure in preventing hail. The manner in which the offerings burn indicates whether or not they have been accepted. Then all eat and drink at the expense of the *jilakata*.

Another less frequent function of the section magician is rain production. This entails bringing water from a certain spring down from the top of Jipi, the highest mountain in the Compi area. This is considered to be a particularly dangerous task. Alcohol must be given to the Jipi spirit to "pay" him for the water but it must not be imbibed by the magician himself, for alcohol is associated with fire and might consume the water, creating an even more severe drought. Compeños tell a story about a particularly negligent *achachila* who was confronted by Segundino, an old-time magician from Cawaya who still practiced the rare art of conversing with the spirits through ventriloquism or change of voice in spirit sessions. One year rains began to fall only late in January instead of in November-December. Segundino ascertained through divination that the *achachila* had gone off to Potosí to attend his daughter's wedding. When the *achachila* finally returned Segundino "whipped" and scolded him and forced him to "drink" pure alcohol during a seance until the *achachila* excused himself for his absence and promised to produce rain again. Soon afterwards, heavy rains did indeed fall.

Ritual mediation between the natural and supernatural spheres is called for on a number of other occasions as well.

Mesas or sacrifices are offered to the spirits after voluntary and involuntary abortion, stillbirths, abnormal births and multiple births. These atypical occurrences are paralleled by illness and foul weather in the form of hail and strong winds, the reverse of the natural state of health, normal birth, and favorable skies. In a ceremony after the birth of twins and their subsequent death, the giving of offerings was accompanied by a ceremony whereby persons within the community begged each other's pardon. The offerings reestablished normality on the supernatural level just as the asking of pardon reintegrated the community. Normality on the human level is extended to that of the spirits through the media of ritual offerings.

In another instance, the umbilical cord is disposed of in the lake or river in order that "the household continue." The umbilical cord, the symbol of human continuity, is offered to the lake/river spirits who are symbols of natural continuity.

Alcohol and coca are also important offerings in all rites, especially in the *rutucha* (the ceremony accompanying the first haircut) and in the feast of All Saints', which we shall analyze at the end of this section.

Another ritual method of bridging the two spheres is "exchange." The following case may serve as an example of this method. An informant explained that when her son Felix failed to crawl, she asked a *yatiri*, a curer, to heal him with a guinea pig. He put the dead guinea pig on the foot of the child, which was to be "exchanged." The Spanish *"hacen cambiar,"* translated here "to be exchanged," means that the curer magically offered an object, in this case a guinea pig, to God in lieu of a human being, that is, Felix. The guinea pig was named Felix. Then the animal and incense were offered as a favor to God, for perhaps the retardation was a punishment of God. But, by the same token, a quality of the object was magically transferred to the human, that is, the ability to move.

Intermediaries span the two spheres as well. In the story "The Condor and Lorenzo," the hummingbird, a supernatural, acts as an intermediary in relating messages from the mother, a human, to the Condor, a supernatural, in the form of an animal who has captured her daughter.

We have shown how ritual measures, offerings, "exchange" and intermediaries are an extension of the individual or group. Ritual determines "the message." In the cases cited above it serves as a vehicle for the expression of the principles which govern Aymara thought processes. This interrelationship of human growth, nature and the supernatural can be depicted best in the events of All Saints' Day and the *rutucha*.

During All Saints', the interrelationship of the three spheres of life is demonstrated in the following way. On the commemorative altar, many symbolic offerings represent or are specially destined for dead infants and old men. As we have seen, children play an important part in All Saints', in the ceremony for the dead. The beginning and the end of life are close; fertility and death are mirror images of one reality. Death characterizes both old age and early childhood in this society. Boys sing to the spirits of the dead: "You have come to water the flowers," in other words, to insure growth. Children, growing humans, intercede for the growth of nature. Little girls and young unmarried women dance with borrowed babies or dolls in their carrying shawls. These dolls are symbolic of continuity too, as they are said to attract the souls of dead children and insure the future fertility of the girls. Finally, during the profane part of All Saints', the contact between the two spheres of humans and spirits is broken by a series of reversals, mentioned previously.

Ritual is the "instant vision of a complex process," according to McLuhan. In the *rutucha* we can not only see the complex process but we will present once more the three phases of our analysis: the relationship between mental constructs and social structure, the principles which govern the foregoing, and the analysis of ritual and magicians. On one level the *rutucha* may be seen as a means of incorporating the child into the social network of the community. Ties of ritual kinship are established as well as ties of economic reciprocity for the parents, and the child as he matures, is obligated to return the gifts of food, money, and so on at the feasts of their guests. On another level the *rutucha* expresses the

Aymara Weltanschauung: the supernatural world is closely related to nature, and since humans and the natural sphere are likewise closely related so the supernatural human and natural phenomena are frequently intertwined. The growth of the child is symbolized by the growth of produce and money. Money represents land or trucks. (Trucks are necessary to bring crops to La Paz.) At one point the godfather says "May the plate of our godchild grow so large that he can buy trucks and land," for the child is to enjoy these gifts as an adult. The gifts of money and produce are sprinkled with alcohol with which one libates the Earth Mother. One libates the earth to ensure fertility, the increase of the earth's produce. Thus the maize, the Earth Mother's produce, money as the symbol of plenty, and the child's potential growth into a man "as valiant as his godfather" are all interrelated. On yet another level one could analyze the *rutucha* in terms of principles of identity and oppositions, that is, the growth of the child is paralleled by the growth of produce, at the same time the cutting of hair is related to the increase in fertility. The magician's presence is essential in endorsing the ceremony.

The entire community preoccupies itself with the question of twins especially when one or both of them die. A good example of this was the *despacho* of twins who had been born dead in Kalamaya. On December 14th, 1965, we were told that the week before twins had been born dead. It was a boy and a girl, which signified misery. They were buried without the ceremonial "disposition." When it hailed on Monday, December 12th, the family became alarmed. The people knew about the birth but because the family was poor, they had done nothing. On Tuesday, the 13th of December, they had begun a large ceremony. They called four *yatiris*, or *maestros*, from Tauca and from Compi because the *maestros* from Kalamaya do not know how to dispose of twins ceremonially. (They know only how to do the more elementary magic like giving hail *mesas*.) Each maestro was assigned to different tasks. They prepared the *mesas* and searched for "*los niños apostoles*," that is, six boys and six girls representing the twelve apostles of Christ. These children had to present some abnormal trait, some could be born feet first, others have six toes on their feet or webbed hands, yet others could be twins or *sonakes*, children who have hair growing unnaturally from two centers or who have it parted in two sides which is called "two heads." Others could be orphans. When twelve such abnormal children had been found, they were made to pray for the entire night. First they made the sign of the cross, then they prayed Our Father, the Hail Mary, the Benediction, the Gloria, prayers of confession and the Creed. Each time the *maestro*, a prayer reciter rather than a magician proper, began, and the children repeated the words after him. They were not allowed to eat anything during the night except for some bread and wine at 12 P.M. (probably signifying the Holy Communion). In the morning they were given ground maize. We arrived at 10:30 A.M. The children were praying for the last time. They were all sitting in two rows in the center of the patio of the family who had lost the twins, facing the door of the main hut. With them was the *maestro*. At a given signal the *maestro* began praying, the children kneeling, repeated the prayers after him. Later the other *maestros* prepared various *mesas*.[2] One included ground in-

---

[2] Mesas: offerings of various articles for magical rites.

cense, another yarn wound in reverse and the third contained things necessary for a *Chhiuchhi mesa*: *Chhiuchhis* (small lead figures), multicolored wool, the fat of various animals, scraped white stones and wildcat's fur. One had a living black guinea pig in a bag which was to be "exchanged" for the sins and the grief of the community, so that no disgrace would befall either the village or the mother of the twins. To safeguard all concerned, the *maestros* passed from one person to another, holding the bundles over the head of each person present while praying and exhorting the spirits. This was repeated with the flowers and the other bundles as well as with two rotten eggs.[3] One of the *maestros* also tore threads of three colors; black, dogs', cats' and guinea pigs' wool; white llama wool; and red llama wool, spun the wrong way, over the heads of the persons. Black means grief, so all the curses would be dispelled by breaking the thread. White signifies good health and so does red, the latter being for the health of the souls. *Kantutas*, the Bolivian national flower, were used to remove sorrow. The rotten eggs were used so that twins would never be born again and to prevent hail. Some persons would ask the *maestros* for special favors. For instance, one person told the *maestro* that his back was hurting, so the *maestro* passed over his back the black guinea pig so that the pain could be exchanged for the guinea pig which would later be carried up to the hills.

At this point, the three persons who were nominated to take the *mesas* up on the hills, left the compound. Apart from the bundles with the *mesas*, they took all the clothing which had been soiled by blood at the birth of the twins and even the garbage and straw which had been in the house in which the birth took place. This was done in order to remove all sorrow from the house and thus from the community. They also took along the bunches of flowers which all the men and women had brought. With these the villagers had purified their houses from sorrow, and to remove pain from the community they sent it along with the three men. One woman, for instance, held three *Kantutas* tied with white yarn which was also spun in reverse. One was for herself, one for her husband, and one for her son. Some persons arrived late, when the men had already left for the hills with their bundles. Those present were very much displeased with these late comers for in this way their flowers could not be sent to the hills and thus much sorrow would still remain in the community. In any case the *maestros* "blessed" all with the different items.

Then, at about 12 A.M. the actual ceremony began. By this time almost the entire community was present, or at least some representative of each family. Usually both the family head, his wife and some children were present. The parents of the twins were made to kneel in front of the cross. Each parent was handed an incense burner by the *yatiri* and his aide. The incense was provided by close relatives. The parents asked for pardon as they swung the incense burner toward the crucifix. The grandmother cried, "What punishment have you brought upon us?" Florentino, the oldest man in the community, known for his knowledge of Catholic prayers and hymns, led the ceremony. First he sang *"Dulce Señor,"* (Sweet Savior),

---

[3] One always keeps rotten eggs at home for magic: for example, one throws them behind two persons in order to seed discord between them, naming the persons on whom one wants to put a spell.

Magicians purifying the community after the death of twins.

then *Madre de Señor*" (Mother of God), and finally the Benedictus. The Ten Commandments, the seven sacraments, and the preparation for the communion were also recited. All this was repeated in chorus by the assembled community.

Then, each member of the family of the twins came up to the altar to give incense. They knelt man, wife and child as a *yatiri* gave each a bowl with live embers and incense. They turned the bowl from left to right which meant that sorrow would leave them and the spirit of the lake would help the relatives of the twins: "If one asks anything of the spirit of the lake one addresses him as his grandchildren or his orphans." One also begs Christ as orphans in order to be pitied. The *maestro* who led the "*niños apostoles*" made them pray once more.

After this, led by the family, all the persons present asked for pardon from each other. One by one they passed through the rows of kneeling villagers embracing them and saying "Pardon me for all the offenses I have committed." The person from whom pardon was requested answered: "God will forgive you." They even asked us and the children present for pardon. The "*niños apostles*" did the same at the end but silently. They then entered the house and were given food after their long fast. Food was served to all. All the women who came brought cooked food, a custom observed in all family ceremonies. We left at this point, but the feast continued until the *yatiris* returned from the hill with news of whether the offering had been accepted by the spirits or not. Acceptance or rejection of the offering is indicated by the color of the smoke; white is favorable, black unfavorable. The wild animals met on the way are also considered omens. A male *alkamari* (a black and white bird of prey) is supposed to be a good sign, a fox or an owl a bad one. Similarly if one crosses paths with a man it is a good sign, if with a woman it is a bad one.

Paradox marks the attitude toward twins. On the one hand they are respected as "loved ones of God" but on the other hand, they are feared as signs of God's displeasure, for they "are destined for the spirits." However, fear is only expressed when the proper ceremonial rites are *not* observed. For the unusual event of twins, symbolized by rotten eggs, yarn spun the wrong way, and so on, may be accompanied by unusual events in nature, that is, hail or strong winds. To avoid these, people respect and avoid quarreling with twins: "The people say one should neither maltreat nor insult twins or one will fall into disgrace." One must not scold the family of twins either. It is *ñanka* (it will cause one to fracture a hand or head). So adults and children alike treat twins with care. They never "fight them nor let them cry."

Twins are said to love each other very much. They are sometimes dressed alike. The family of twins, if they are poor, are given food even in the rainy season when food is scarce. "One feels for them." "All must ask forgiveness for them." Nevertheless certain precautions have to be taken: they should not suckle at their mother's breasts at the same time, and they should be carried facing away from each other, or else they will fight with each other when they grow older.

Ambivalent attitudes mark the birth of deformed infants as well. The following deformations were related to us: children with six toes or fingers (*pulu pulu*), webbed fingers (*karachi*), birth marks, children born with eyes open, deformed legs and arms, club feet. These children are said to be "beloved of God." That is perhaps the reason why they are asked to intercede at the atonement ceremony of the twins. At their birth one gives incense too, just in case their abnormality may be reflected in nature.

The ritual connected with the death of the donkey also illustrates the interaction between the natural and supernatural. It follows a similar pattern to the twin ceremony except for the exclusion of the communal part of the ceremony. An offering was prepared by a magician which included a number of black and white pebbles. The same ceremonial cleansing of those present was observed when two men left for the mountain top to burn the offering. The magician, an old-timer, put up a most impressive show. He whipped the courtyard with a whip with abandoned fury to cleanse it of all evil spirits. Then he climbed the hill slope where the donkey had been deposited earlier. Only a handful of adolescent boys had the courage to follow him. There he split the stomach of the donkey repeatedly so that the gas forming inside would not burst the stomach and continued his invocations to pacify the mountain spirits, tearing strands of yarn spun in reverse and sprinkling alcohol with his fingers.

Curing

In the preceding pages we have repeatedly referred to the *maestro* or *yatiri*, the magician. This specialist should be differentiated from the *curandero* or curer who heals with herbs, although many magicians are curers as well. Both men and women learn their trade by apprenticeship and may become specialists in magic or herbal lore. An unusual experience, such as Quintin's serious illness mentioned earlier, may be the initial impetus for specialization. Curers are paid for their services and attend persons in their own and neighboring communities.

Both natural and supernatural causes are ascribed to disease. Natural causes include faulty care, while supernatural ones may include the loss of soul or possession by an evil force. Flora told us the following tale: "When my child felt ill, they thought it was a place that caused her illness. So they went to a place where there is a stone in the shape of a horse which the child had mounted previous to the illness. We knelt and gave *mesas*, but the child died anyway. Maybe it was eaten."

Illnesses may be caused by *susto*, or fright. Anytime during the day or night one may be frightened by an animal or an apparition of an animal such as a dog or a donkey. A person might fall ill with a headache or of an illness of the hands, feet, ears, or eyes. The *yatiri*, or curer, should be called in such a situation in order to recall the *animo*,[4] one of the three souls a person possesses. This is accomplished in the following manner. A piece of the patient's clothing is laid on the ground a short distance from the patient's house by the *maestro*. He is accompanied by at least one friend or a relative of the patient. Near the patient's clothing is put the contents of llama entrails, gall stones diluted in holy water in a little cup, with St. Nicholas bread (a sort of wafer with the image of St. Nicholas) and *chinchi chinchi* (unidentified fruit). Then they both retreat to the house. After this, the curer calls to and libates the *animo* with alcohol. In the meantime, the patient is supposed to sleep in order for the soul to reenter its abode. (Sleep may be considered an intermediary between life and death.) While waiting for the soul's return during the patient's sleep, other *animos* may appear. These are the *animos* of persons who will fall ill in the near future, and can be clearly identified. When the patient's *animo* arrives it has to be enveloped immediately in the clothing. They (the curer and his assistant) then place the clothing beside the patient, making him drink some of the holy water and wash his face. Then they put the clothing on the patient. During the process of calling the soul, wool spun in reverse is also used. One tears small pieces and throws them to the wind, calling the soul as one throws. The next day this wool is burned and the patient must drink the ashes mixed with water. Yarn spun in reverse is also placed in the patient's hands and on the ground around him so that the soul may not escape. If the patient does not recover, this may be due to complications with other spirits, such as a lake, or other *achachila*, or *rayo* (lightning or site where lightning has struck). A *mesa* (burnt offering) has to be given on the site where the person experienced a *susto*, or at the site where lightning has struck. However, *susto* may also be cured by natural herbal remedies such as a brew of *ithapi* (unidentified), *chinchi chinchi* or *chhojjlla* (grass).

As we have seen, illness is caused by both natural and supernatural phe-

---

[4] According to other *yatiris* the *ajayu*, a second soul, is the soul which is lost. The third soul is a person's *coraje* (or "courage").

nomena. So it is treated accordingly. For whooping cough one is supposed to bathe the child in water with a concoction of eucalyptus leaves or other herbal teas like *moleta* (unidentified), *marancilla* leaves (*Clarionae atacamensis*), *tonko tonko* (corn silk), *panti panti* (cosmos sp.). In case of diarrhoea one prescribes *chacu chacu* (unidentified). One uses linseed and starch for dysentery and *susto*. For *c'ajja* (cough) one puts fat on the throat, rubs it with dirty black sheep's wool and gives syrup. But *mallk'u* or scarlet fever is treated supernaturally by going to a hill near Huarina. There one grinds the stone of the hill and puts it on the skin of the child: for the face of the hill is similar to the skin of a child with scarlet fever. Finally, one may buy aspirin or a drug against intestinal worms from the missionary nurse who comes to the Jank'o Amaya market once a week.

*

      *   *

Early twentieth century scholars (for example, Dürkheim and Freud) tended to adopt the point of view that primitive peoples viewed their relationship with natural phenomena or animal species as one of identification and causality. For example, a clan was said to establish a relationship of religious or magical dependency and identity with an animal or plant species. Radcliffe-Brown and Lévi-Strauss were among the first to realize that the association of different segments of a society with different "totems" simply was a language in which the distinctness of these segments could be expressed.[5] For instance, in Australia the differences between such animal species as kangaroos and wombats serve as a metaphor to distinguish two clans.

The manner in which the Aymara structure the universe follows such a pattern of correspondence between different spheres. It is not because samples of the stony slopes of a certain hillside have magical powers that they are supposed to heal a child with scarlet fever, but because the grinding of such stones is expected to have a corresponding transformation of the diseased skin. It is not because fetuses cause hail that the Aymara are apprehensive about abortions, but because the act of interrupting the normal development of a child in the community may find a parallel in nature when hail impedes the normal maturation of the crops. In other words, in order to attain a balance between the forces of nature, a complementary normality in reproduction must be maintained. Confession reestablishes the normal relationship of the mother with the community. Bringing the fetus to the top of a hill removes it from the sphere of the society to the supernatural, where reaction is blocked by sacrifices.

We have emphasized the relationship of the natural and the supernatural in both ritual and curing. The reader will have noted that repeatedly both Aymara and Roman Catholic religious elements were intertwined. For the role of formal Catholic rites and of Protestantism we refer to the chapter on fiestas to complete the description of religion in Compi.

---

[5] For an analysis of these theories, see Lévi-Strauss 1963.

8

Conclusion

IN THE PREFACE WE STATED that certain patterns of interaction or network regularities persist under a variety of conditions and may aid a society in adapting to changing situations or may even promote change. As we have seen, Compi exemplifies a number of these patterns. One of the most adaptable behavior complexes in Aymara society is the family, which we have defined as a series of circles of relationships. Family flexibility manifests itself in migration and marketing. While the Compi households are growing smaller, the ties between close relatives have not disappeared, they have simply been reallocated to fulfill different functions such as providing lodgings and outlets for produce for Compeños on their market trips to La Paz. Thus, while assuming a different geographical dimension, the extended family still retains paramount importance in Compi social structure. As we have shown, these continuing relationships made their impact upon the community and county levels as well. Returned migrants provided more adequate leadership suited to deal with the reform programs of the national government, and merchants, familiar with the wider economic channels, furnished local markets with consumer goods. The networks of social relationships made possible through ties with migrants can thus be seen not only as an adaptation to changing situations but as a mechanism promoting change as well.

We noted similar processes with respect to community and county structure. The history of Compi revealed constantly changing relationships between its sections and between the community and the county. These section relationships were readjusted as the hacienda Compi grew to the detriment of the free community Llamacachi and as the newly acquired sections were integrated into the administrative structure of the hacienda. Later they acquired a series of new relationships with the abolition of the hacienda system, the struggle to acquire titles to the land, and the construction of a joint school. On the county level this flexibility manifested itself in the disintegration of the county of Santiago de Huata and the competition of communities vying for the position of county capital. The changing relationships of section, community, and county were, as we have indicated, directly related to changing leadership patterns and to changes in social stratification. In a sense the entire political history of Compi can be seen in the light of both the confrontation and intersection of a system based on decision by consensus by men who are linked in a dense network through descent, marriage, neighborhood, and to a lesser extent through friendship and ritual kin ties, coupled with a social hierarchy dependent on seniority and prestige acquired by serving the community, with another system based on appointments by higher officials.

Flexibility of social forms in turn allowed for variety. Compi was chosen for study not because it is "average," "traditional," or "progressive," but because widely divergent leadership patterns, relationships to the ruling class, and processes of change were present. For instance if we had studied leadership patterns in only one section, Compi proper, we would have obtained quite a different impression of Aymara politics than if our choice had been Capilaya or Llamacachi.

Had we chosen another Bolivian Aymara community for our study we would have encountered additional patterns. For instance, migratory patterns differ from place to place. Thus in free communities on the peninsula of Santiago de Huata, less than ten miles from Compi, a large number of men work regularly in the sub-tropical Yungas valleys. Across the lake, on the peninsula of Copacabana, men specialize in selling jerked llama meat in the Yungas and dealing with coca leaves which they sell in La Paz. Many have established themselves permanently in the Yungas.

The history of two migrant families will serve to illustrate this diversity of migratory patterns. The first migrated to an ancient colonization area in the Yungas, and the second to an area which has been settled during the last 15 years or so.

Tomas from Calaque, for instance, came to work in Charobamba, a hacienda near Coroico, when he was a boy and later stayed to work as a permanent laborer there. Both sets of parents arranged that he marry a Calaqueña. After the agrarian reform, he received land in Charobamba and settled down permanently. Tomas' father-in-law comes to help every year for two months or so. Another relative of his wife's visits them frequently and stays at their home on his business trips. During the past few years a cousin of his and an unrelated Calaqueño are working for him also. However, unlike some of his fellow migrants, he does not visit his home community any longer, nor do his relatives send him produce although he theoretically is still entitled to some land.

In the newly colonized areas, contacts with relatives on the altiplano are still more important than in the upper part of the Yungas valleys. Since land is more plentiful in these areas, houses are often far apart; moreover, communities are often composed of persons of different origins who scarcely know each other. Due to a scarcity of labor the colonists depend on outside sources of labor for many agricultural tasks. The easiest way to secure labor is to avail oneself of the assistance of relatives and other *paisanos*.

Another good example is Damaso Apasa. He came from Chiquipata to the colonization area around Caranavi with his family some ten years ago, enticed by a false promise that the government would provide tools for migrants. He recalls that there were no roads in the area at that time. He began by working for a patrón and then started his own coffee, banana, and papaya plantations. At first he worked alone, but at present his nephews from the altiplano are helping him for two or three weeks at a time. Other relatives come to lend a hand also. One nephew, for instance, settled in the area after having worked for Damaso for a month while looking for vacant land. But Damaso's sons do not intend to remain in the Yungas as farmers. Like many of their *paisanos* they wish to live in La Paz and deal with Yungas produce. Damaso himself still owns land in his home community which his daughter cultivates. They exchange produce when they meet in La Paz. He himself visits Chiquipata on the altiplano only once a year for three or four weeks for the community's largest fiesta.

Even in those communities where peasants migrated to the same place as Compeños, that is, to La Paz, migratory patterns differ. While Compi men have taken up a variety of occupations in La Paz, migrants from two free communities in the peninsula of Copacabana have definite preferences. Many migrants from one community have become tailors, those from another bakers.

The relationships between section and community also take many forms. Small communities may not be divided into sections at all and larger ones may be more tightly integrated. For instance, while in Compi each section is politically almost completely independent from the other sections, in Jank'o Amaya all six of its sections form a single syndicate in which each section is represented. Community-county relationships vary as well. In Calaque, a very large free community which once belonged to the same county as Llamacachi, competition for the county seat took place between sections of the same community rather than between communities as in the case of Compi. Thus county politics may affect internal unity as well as external ties.

The relationship between peasant officials and the hacienda administration as well as the county government may also vary. In many haciendas there were no *sot'as* and the *jilakatas* were often appointed annually, on the recommendations of the community elders who in turn based their decisions on similar criteria as those of free communities, that is, fiesta sponsorship and fulfillment of lower political office rather than being appointed for an indefinite period of time according to the whims of the patrón as was the case in Compi. In these cases hacienda services, such as shepherd, were simply incorporated in the list of prerequisites for higher leadership positions.

In contrast to Llamacachi where the *jilakata's* obligations to the county judge became so burdensome that the community abandoned recruitment according to the sole criteria of the prestige system, in many communities the traditional political ladder remained unaffected.

In post-reform times the differences in leadership patterns were even more remarkable. In some communities syndicate leaders and/or school directors gained more powers than their counterparts in Compi. Similarly, peasant leaders on the province level were much more influential in some areas than in others.

Organizational differences in turn reflect themselves in ritual. For instance, the fact that Jank'o Amaya sections are more cohesive than Compi sections is reflected in the fact that dance groups composed of dancers of more than one section are more frequent in Jank'o Amaya than in Compi. Furthermore the same section does not usually furnish a *preste* for two consecutive years but there is no fixed sequence in which sections provide sponsors as there is in Compi. More elementary ritual rules may vary as well. Compeños are well aware of such differences in custom and comment on them frequently.

Nevertheless these differences are based on the same regularities of behavior. For instance the same flexible family relationships underlie migratory patterns on the peninsula of Santiago de Huata and Copacabana as those of Compeños. While migrants from diverse localities have individual preferences as to destination and profession, the means whereby they acquire their positions and their relationship to the community of origin are similar. For instance, like many Compeños, people from Amakari and Oje on the peninsula of Copacabana very frequently obtain their jobs through relatives. Thus in Amakari a man established himself as a tailor in La Paz. Later others followed suit, many apprenticing themselves with relatives. The fact that many more migrants chose the same profession than in Compi can be accounted for by the fact that Amakareños, being *comunidad* peasants, could choose the time of migration, while in Compi the mass exodus brought about by hacienda policies forced the *colonos* to seek jobs on their own account instead of relying mainly on relatives.

The comparison of migration to La Paz and migration to the Yungas valleys is of particular interest. In spite of the fact that the migrant faces completely different conditions in the Yungas and in La Paz, the types of ties between the migrants and their families are very similar. The main difference lies in the fact that, in the case of migrants to the Yungas, labor is required in the community of destination rather than in the community of origin, for labor is scarce in the Yungas and thousands of seasonal laborers from the altiplano are needed during critical periods in the agricultural cycle.

The desire to gain political and/or economic ascendance over neighboring communities is a common trend present on both the high plateau and the Yungas, with the establishment of a county seat generally considered the best means to attain this end. While grassroot politics vary from place to place they too take similar shapes. The pre-reform position of the *jilakatas* on haciendas was inherently ambiguous. Pre-reform relations between owners and administrators on the one hand and county judges on the other took the form of some mutual understanding restricting the influence of the judges in hacienda matters, even though the understanding was coupled with latent antagonism. In contrast, free community authorities were more strongly dependent on county judges although they retained a high degree of autonomy in local concerns. Finally, fiesta rules may vary but all are based on a sponsorship-prestige-reciprocity system which provides a ritual language comprehensible to highland peasants as well as townsmen and Pazeños.

The flexibility of Aymara social forms and Aymara-creole relationships extends to the cities. In our presentation we made no strict dichotomy between rural and urban phenomena; for the migrant population and their descendants remain in constant contact with villages and rural communities. Migrants go out to local fairs and fiestas, or to help cultivate plots of land to which they have retained access while peasants stay at their relatives' home in La Paz when they visit to sell produce or to bring a small share of the harvest. So family ties remain important, although the circles are widened to include Pazeños and migrants from other areas. We noted that a high percentage of marriages are contracted with persons from the same area. Furthermore, political functions of migrants integrate the La Paz governmental structure and local leadership in a single system in which the individual peasant has the choice of presenting his case either in the community, in the county, or in various governmental offices in La Paz.

If we go farther afield and compare Compi community structure and migratory patterns with those of highland communities in Ecuador, similar social forms altered to fit different circumstances may be seen. For instance, in the province of Cotopaxi where the authors did fieldwork, the Spaniards had established an administrative structure similar to that of the Bolivian altiplano. However, ruling class control over the indigenous population is more encompassing than in Bolivia. Huaytacama, an Ecuadorian parish in Cotopaxi, can be considered as the administrative equivalent of an altiplano county. It is composed of six free communities, or *barrios* (classified by Ecuadorians as Indian as opposed to *mestizo*), seven large cattle haciendas, and a small centrally located group of *mestizos* and wealthier Indians living in a nucleated settlement. In Huaytacama there is almost no corporate action on the *barrio* level, rather, the *barrios* are almost entirely dependent on three spheres of political influence, the parish priest; the *teniente politico*, a *mestizo* official appointed by the Ecuadorian government, and the haciendas upon which even the free communities depend for a living.

The parish priest acts as an informal judge, guards over the morals of the parishioners, controls two of the four schools, and calls corvées to construct schools and churches and to clean streets. The *teniente politico*, a government appointed official, acts as formal judge and also calls corvées for public works. Both nominate officials from the *barrios* who rarely act on their own accord, since they are completely dependent on the orders of the priest and of the *teniente politico*. Moreover, a considerable proportion of the population, especially those of poorer *barrios,* depends on the neighboring cattle haciendas for a large part of their income. Thus, whereas Llamacachi's economy was quite independent of neighboring Compi, the hacienda is an integral part of the economy of the *barrios* in Huaytacama. The agrarian reform initiated by the military junta in 1964 changed the situation but little. Small parcels of land were apportioned to peasants living on hacienda land and salaries were increased slightly, but the agrarian structure of large landowners and poor peasants has remained the same. A government program dating back to the thirties to develop local leadership has been reinstated by the Andean Mission. However, in Huaytacama, this endeavor has failed almost completely. Thus, in Huaytacama, outside influences seem to have created both a socio-religious system which completely enveloped former organizational patterns as well as new larger administrative units, the parishes which have become the endogamous units rather than the community as in the Bolivian altiplano. On the contrary, in Compi local organization was not completely engulfed, not even by the hacienda system. Viable local leadership was therefore easily reinstalled once the hacienda system was abolished.

Migration is even more important in Huaytacama than it is in Compi. Few families can subsist on the yield of their plots of land alone. Marriage records show that, at least since the second part of the nineteenth century, Huaytacameños have been occupied in a variety of professions. In addition to work on landed estates all poorer families weave reed mats or cotton belts. Others supplement agriculture by working as tailors, hatters, middlemen, storekeepers, and so on. But work within the parish is insufficient for the subsistence of a large proportion of Huaytacameños, both wealthy and poor. Adults and children work on *pyrethrum* (a plant from which an insecticide is produced, and which grows in cold regions) plantations. Young men migrate to coastal plantations for one to three months at a time or deal in clothing and other items. Women rarely migrate to the coast since little land seems to be available, the majority of it being owned by the plantations. Instead, they cultivate the family lands, or act as vendors in local markes and in Quito. Others, especially unmarried girls work as servants either in Latacunga, a small city nearby, or in Quito. There seems to be no general preference in the parish as to place of migration or for any one occupation outside of the *barrio*. Rather each person may take up a variety of activities in different places on the coast, the eastern slopes of the Andes, and in highland haciendas, villages, towns, and cities. Although their social network is much vaster than that of Compeños, family ties still play an important function, providing companionship during seasonal work in other places and a firm link with the place of origin which is usually visited every one to three months. In cities like Quito relatives of migrants living in the same city are invited to family feasts and relatives from the home community are given lodgings. Successful merchants or craftsmen who have returned to Huaytacama are improving their houses in emulation of *mestizo* peasants, creating a definite stratification within the parish. Leaders chosen by the parish priest and the *teniente politico* frequently come from this class. However, since they do not act as independent leaders but merely follow orders of their superiors, their influence on the community is not considerable. Recently for instance, one of the *barrios* of Huaytacama became the focus of activities of the Andean Mission. After initial success, the project in this *barrio*, which depended on a few returned migrants, slowly disintegrated. Lack of time due to work on haciendas and lack of confidence in future improvement have discouraged most Indian peasants from working on Andean Mission projects.

In both Compi and Huaytacama then, territorial boundaries do not adequately describe the community. In both, returning migrants act as intermediaries between peasants and government officials. But while migration led to the formation of stronger peasant leadership in Compi, it led to pronounced social stratification in Huaytacama which has split the community, rendering joint action even more difficult than before.

The description of social organization within Compi and Llamacachi's administrative boundaries cannot provide us with a blueprint for the study of the Andean area, the Aymara, or even the county of which the community forms a part, nor does the present duplicate the past. In order to discover regularities of behavior in the changing and variable situations which characterize the Andes, the anthropologist must go beyond artificial and self-imposed geographic, social, ethnic, and temporal boundaries. Rather—within the practical limits of participant observation and ethnohistory—he must follow the network of social relationships through time and space. The analysis of such networks through history and comparisons with other regions reveal similarities in behavioral patterns despite widely divergent contexts. Some of these similarities lie in family relationships, others in marriage patterns, or in local politics and factionalism; some are associated with the bridging of different ecological zones, others with the adaptation of Andean peasants to their Inca and Spanish overlords. All are amazingly flexible, defying any simple definition and categorization. Such a comparative network approach may lead to a better understanding of both the dynamics of change and variation and of continuities in behavior patterns.

Glossary

achachila: mountain or lake spirit.

achokalla: home roofing celebration (syn. *utachiri*).

aini: (1) reciprocal labor, and lending and borrowing, the latter especially in connection with fiestas. (2) the persons involved.

alcalde: (1) official during hacienda times who seconded the *jilakata* (see below). (2) parallel official in free communities important in agricultural rites.

alcalde escolar: school official in charge of making the school breakfast, organizing school festivals and attending meetings where problems concerning the school are discussed.

altarero: minor sponsor in fiestas.

altiplano: high plateau of Bolivia and Southern Peru.

asuti: ceremony performed by adolescents when a child is born.

awayo: carrying shawl in which women transport both children and produce.

cabecilla: minor dance group sponsor and dance leader.

cabeza: major dance group sponsor.

caceras: women involved in a commercial relationship.

camani(a): person assigned to making *chuño* in hacienda times.

cantón: (1) smallest administrative unit above the community. (2) the capital of such a unit usually a nucleated settlement with a weekly market and offices for a judge and a notary public, sometimes also a telegraph service.

cargo: feast sponsorship.

c'aya: frozen and dried *oca* (see below).

chhamaka preste: man responsible for the ceremony honoring a recently deceased relative during All Saints'.

chino: a bottle of alcohol tied with a square cloth containing coca given as a deposit to future sponsors in fiestas, dancers, etc.

chiquiña: furrows of land in each plot possessed by the head of a family, given on a temporary basis to close relatives of the head of the family (especially sisters and daughters), usually in return for their help in agricultural activities.

chola: upwardly mobile migrant wearing silk peasant style clothing.

chuño: frozen and dried potatoes.

colono: peasant or serf who worked for a landowner in return for a plot of land (pre-reform).

comadre: ritual kin term used to express the tie established between a godmother of a child at baptism, the *rutucha*, or wedding, and the parents and close relatives of the child.

compadre: male equivalent of *comadre*.

comunidad: free community not subject to landowners previous to the agrarian reform.

comunario: peasant from a free community.

corregidor: (1) in hacienda times *mestizo* who ruled a cantón. (2) presently, aide to the *intendente*, (See below).

dispensero: person in charge of the food and storage room of a major fiesta sponsor.

ex-colono: term frequently employed for peasant from a former land estate.

ex-hacienda: term employed for a land estate after the agrarian reform.

haba: broad bean, one of the major crops around Lake Titicaca.

hacienda: landed estate which was cultivated by a system of serfdom until the system was eradicated by the agrarian reform of 1953.

imilla: female child.

intendente: head of a cantón, with judicial and police functions, develops public utilities in the cantón capital.

jilakata: (1) in former haciendas, task master directing work on hacienda land under the direction of the administrator and the *sot'as* (see below). (2) today, head of free communities; second in charge in ex-haciendas.

kachua: rite of adolescents performed on Saint Andrew's (Nov. 29th), Saint Lucia (Dec. 13th), and Christmas.

kantuta: Bolivian national flower used frequently in magical practices.

maestro: curer or magician, also called *yatiri.*

majordomo: hacienda administrator.

mayoruni: category of hacienda serf with little land.

mesa: burnt offering presented to the achachilas (see above).

mestizo: the term is used here to designate individuals whose lifeways are more strongly influenced by Spanish tradition than those of average Lake Titicaca peasants, for instance they use Spanish as their principal language, but who have not reached the upper circles of Bolivian society.

oca: oxalis crenata (or tuberosa), a root crop second only in importance around Lake Titicaca to the potato.

paisano: inhabitant or migrant from the same community.

paseo: ritualized Sunday promenade in La Paz.

patrón: landowner of pre-reform times.

presidente de la junta vecinal: (1) school authority above the *alcalde escolar* (see above). (2) in Llamacachi, head of the community.

preste: most important sponsor in the fiesta system.

quinua: Chenopodium quinoa, a food plant with small grains high in proteins and minerals.

rutucha: haircutting ceremony.

salvia: dance performed by adolescents during certain evenings between Carnival and Saint Peter's.

sayaña: the sum of plots of land (with the exception of those lying in fields with a common rotational pattern) owned by a peasant.

secretario: member of the board of directors of a peasant syndicate.

sot'a: top task master in the hacienda system nominated by the patrón from among his *colonos.*

susto: fright which causes illness.

tambo: open markets in La Paz which serve as centers of distribution for other markets where the trucks unload their cargo directly.

tari: square cloth tied into a bundle to carry coca.

tawako: female adolescent.

usuiri: midwife.

utachiri: See *achokalla.*

utawawa: (1) adopted child usually a close relative. (2) landless family living with a family with enough land and receiving plots in return for labor, often but not necessarily relatives.

waynito: male adolescent (also *wayna*).

yapa (yapita): a little extra given in a commercial transaction.

yatiri: See *maestro.*

yokalla: male child.

Yungas: steep subtropical valleys on the eastern slopes of the Andes.

References and
Recommended Readings

The Aymara

BUECHLER, H. C., 1968, "The Reorganization of Counties in the Bolivian Highlands: An Analysis of Rural-Urban Networks and Hierarchies," in E. Eddy, ed., *Urban Anthropology: Research Perspectives and Strategies*, Southern Anthropological Society Proceedings, No. 2, University of Georgia Press.
————, 1969, "The Social Position of an Ethnographer in the Field," in F. Henry and S. Saberwal, eds., *Stress and Response in Fieldwork*. New York: Holt, Rinehart and Winston, Inc.
————, 1970, "The Ritual Dimension of Rural-Urban Networks: The Fiesta System in the Northern Highlands of Bolivia," in W. Mangin, ed., *Peasants in Cities*. Boston: Houghton-Mifflin Company.
————, and J.-M. Buechler, "Conduct and Code: An Analysis of Market Syndicates and Social Revolution in La Paz, Bolivia," in J. Nash, ed., *Ideology and Social Change in Latin America*. Washington, D.C.: Breech (forthcoming).
CARTER, W. E., 1964, *Agrarian Reform and Aymara Communities*. Gainesville: University of Florida Press.
————, 1968, "Secular Reinforcement in Aymara Death Ritual," *American Anthropologist* 70:238–263.
DEW, E., 1969, *Politics in the Altiplano, the Dynamics of Change in Rural Peru*. Austin: University of Texas Press.
TSCHOPIK, H., 1951, *The Aymara of Chucuito, Peru*. Anthropological Papers of the American Museum of Natural History, Vol. 44, Pt. 2: Vol. 1, *Magic*. New York: American Museum of Natural History.

Network Analysis

The term's first appearance:
BAILEY, F. G., 1963, "Politics and Society in Contemporary Orissa," in C. Philips, ed., *Politics and Society in India*, Studies on Modern Asia and Africa, No. 1. London: G. Allen.
BARNES, J. A., 1954, "Class and Committees in a Norwegian Island Parish," *Human Relations* 7:39–58.

For a theoretical elaboration of the concept:
BARNES, J. A., 1968, "Networks and Political Process," in M. Swartz, ed., *Local-Level Politics*. Chicago: Aldine, pp. 107–130.
BOTT, E. J., 1955, "Urban Families: Conjugal Roles and Social Networks," *Human Relations* 7:345–384.

The concept of interaction flow is a useful complement to network theory:
CHAPPLE, E., and C. Coon, 1942, *Principles of Anthropology*. New York: Holt, Rinehart and Winston, Inc.
For an example of fieldwork techniques to study social networks (see also Buechler 1969):

WHITTEN, N. E., 1970, "Network Analysis and Processes of Adaptation Among Ecuadorian and Nova Scotian Negroes," in M. Freilich, ed., *Marginal Natives: Anthropologists at Work.* New York: Harper & Row, pp. 339–402.

Compradrazgo

For a general introduction to the institution of *compradazgo*:

MINTZ, S. W. and E. Wolf, 1950, "An Analysis of Ritual Godparenthood," *Southwestern Journal of Anthropology,* 6:341–368.

GILLIN, J., 1945. "Moche: A Peruvian Coastal Community." Institute of Social Anthropology, Publication No. 3. Washington, D.C.: Smithsonian Institution.

For other variants of the fiesta system:

ADAMS, R. N., 1959, *A Community in the Andes: Problems and Progress in Muquiyauyo.* Seattle: University of Washington Press, pp. 51–81.

CANCIAN, F., 1965, *Economics and Prestige in a Maya Community: The Religious Cargo System in Zinancantan.* Stanford: Stanford University Press.

CARRAZCO, P., 1961, "The Civil-Religious Hierarchy in Mesoamerican Communities: Pre-Spanish Background and Colonial Development," *American Anthropologist* 63:483–497. Reprinted in Cohen and Middleton, eds., *Comparative Political Systems.* New York: The Natural History Press, 1967.

For an analysis of Aymara character on the basis of a more elaborate death ritual see Carter 1968.

For other interpretations of the fiesta system see Cancian 1965, and:

HARRIS, M., 1964. *Patterns of Race in the Americas.* New York: Walker.

NASH, M., 1958, "Political Relations in Guatemala," *Social and Economic Studies* 7:65–75.

Systems of Thought

LÉVI-STRAUSS, C., 1963, *Totemism.* Boston: Beacon Press.

———, 1966, *The Savage Mind.* Chicago: University of Chicago Press.